IPHONE 15 PRO MAX USER GUIDE

Unlocking the Power and

Potential of Your iPhone 15

Pro Max

Edwin E. Dufresne

TABLE OF CONTENTS

INTRODUCTION

In a world where technology seamlessly blends with our lives, the iPhone 15 Pro Max emerges as a beacon of innovation, promising an unparalleled mobile experience. Prepare to embark on a journey that transcends the boundaries of communication, creativity, and productivity. This comprehensive guide will serve as your trusted companion, unlocking the secrets and potential that lie within your iPhone 15 Pro Max.

As you delve into this guide, you will discover the power to transform your iPhone into an extension of your thoughts, your passions, and your world. Each chapter will unveil a new dimension of possibilities, guiding you through the intricate features and functionalities that make the iPhone 15 Pro Max an exceptional device.

From mastering the art of photography to navigating the boundless realms of the internet, this guide will empower you to become an iPhone virtuoso. You will learn how to personalize your device to reflect your unique style, seamlessly manage your data, and troubleshoot any challenges that may arise.

Whether you are a seasoned tech enthusiast or a novice embarking on your first iPhone adventure, this guide will cater to your every need. Prepare to be captivated by the sheer brilliance of the iPhone 15 Pro Max as you embark on a journey of discovery and limitless possibilities.

CHAPTER 1: EMBARKING ON YOUR IPHONE JOURNEY

Unboxing Your iPhone: A Moment of Revelation

Imagine holding a sleek, pristine box adorned with the iconic Apple logo - the anticipation builds as you prepare to unveil the technological marvel within. The moment has arrived to unbox your iPhone 15 Pro Max, a device that promises to redefine your mobile experience.

With a gentle touch, lift the lid of the box, revealing the immaculately packaged iPhone nestled within its protective casing. The sleek lines and sophisticated design of the device immediately captivate your attention, hinting at the power and innovation it holds.

Carefully remove your iPhone from its packaging, savoring the moment as you hold its smooth, metallic frame for the first time. The weight of the device feels reassuring in your hands, exuding a sense of quality and craftsmanship.

Take a moment to inspect your iPhone closely, admiring its flawless finish and the intricate details that make it a work of art. Run your fingers along the edges, feeling the seamless transition between glass and metal, a testament to Apple's meticulous attention to detail.

As you gaze upon the vibrant display, envision the endless possibilities that await. This is not merely a phone; it's a gateway to a world of communication, creativity, and productivity. Your iPhone 15 Pro Max is ready to become an extension of your thoughts, your passions, and your world.

Powering Up and Setting the Stage

The moment of anticipation has arrived – it's time to breathe life into your iPhone 15 Pro Max and embark on a journey of personalization. With a gentle press of the Side button, the iconic Apple logo illuminates the screen, signaling the awakening of your device.

As the vibrant display springs to life, a sense of excitement fills the air. The iPhone's sleek interface beckons you to explore its depths, promising a world of endless possibilities.

A welcoming setup wizard appears, guiding you through the initial steps of configuring your iPhone. It's a chance to infuse your personality into the device, selecting your preferred language, connecting to Wi-Fi, and creating your unique Apple ID – a passport to the vast Apple ecosystem.

As you navigate through the setup process, you'll discover a myriad of customization options, allowing you to tailor your iPhone experience to your liking. Choose a wallpaper that reflects your style, adjust the sound and vibration settings to your preferences, and enable features that enhance your accessibility.

With each step, your iPhone transforms into a personalized companion, ready to adapt to your needs and preferences. The setup process is not merely a formality; it's an opportunity to forge a connection with your device, setting the stage for a seamless and intuitive user experience.

Creating Your Apple Identity

In the digital realm, your Apple ID serves as a passport to a world of interconnected services and seamless experiences. As you embark on your iPhone 15 Pro Max journey, creating or signing in with your Apple ID unlocks a treasure trove of possibilities.

If you've already ventured into the Apple ecosystem, simply enter your existing Apple ID credentials, and your iPhone will seamlessly integrate with your other Apple devices, bringing your personal data, settings, and preferences into harmony.

For those new to the Apple universe, creating an Apple ID is like opening a door to a realm of endless possibilities. This unique identifier becomes your gateway to the App Store, iCloud, iMessage, FaceTime, and a plethora of other services designed to enrich your digital life.

With your Apple ID, you can seamlessly download apps, access your cloud-stored data, engage in secure and private messaging, and make video calls with crystal-clear clarity. It's not just an account; it's a key that unlocks a world of convenience and interconnectedness.

Whether you're an Apple veteran or a newcomer to this digital ecosystem, your Apple ID serves as a unifying force, connecting your devices, services, and experiences under one umbrella. It's the foundation for a seamless and personalized journey into the world of Apple.

Connecting to the World Wide Web

Imagine holding the vast expanse of the internet in the palm of your hand. With your iPhone 15 Pro Max, connecting to the World Wide Web opens a gateway to limitless information, entertainment, and communication.

As you navigate through the Wi-Fi settings on your iPhone, a list of available networks appears, each representing a portal to the digital realm. Choose your preferred network, enter the password if required, and watch as your iPhone establishes a connection, bridging the gap between your device and the boundless world of online possibilities.

If you're on the go, cellular data becomes your ally, allowing you to maintain a constant connection to the internet wherever your adventures take you. With a simple tap, enable cellular data, and watch as your iPhone seamlessly transitions between Wi-Fi and cellular networks, ensuring uninterrupted access to the digital world.

As you surf the web, your iPhone transforms into a window to a universe of knowledge, news, and entertainment. Explore the depths of Wikipedia, stay abreast of current events, or immerse yourself in captivating videos and music. The internet is your oyster, ready to be explored at your fingertips.

Whether you're seeking information, connecting with loved ones, or simply indulging in a moment of relaxation, your iPhone 15 Pro Max, empowered by Wi-Fi and cellular data, serves as your passport to the digital realm. The world is at your fingertips, waiting to be discovered.

Enriching Your iPhone with Apps

Here is a detailed explanation of how to enrich your iPhone experience with apps:

1. Productivity Apps

- **Evernote:** This app is a great way to capture ideas, create to-do lists, and keep track of important information. You can use it to take notes in meetings, create grocery lists, or even save recipes. Evernote syncs across all your devices, so you can access your notes wherever you go.

- **Google Drive:** Google Drive is a cloud storage service that allows you to store, access, and share files from anywhere. You can use it to store documents, photos, videos, and more. Google Drive is free for up to 15GB of storage, and you can purchase additional storage if needed.

- **Microsoft OneNote:** Microsoft OneNote is a digital notebook that allows you to organize notes, drawings, and audio recordings. You can use it to take notes in class, create meeting minutes, or even plan a trip. OneNote syncs across all your devices, so you can access your notes wherever you go.

- **Notion:** Notion is an all-in-one workspace that allows you to combine notes, tasks, projects, and calendars in one place. You can use it to manage your personal and professional life. Notion is free for personal use, and you can purchase a subscription for more features.

- **Trello:** Trello is a project management tool that uses a visual Kanban board system. You can use it to manage projects of any size, from personal to professional. Trello is free for personal use, and you can purchase a subscription for more features.

2. Learning Apps

- **Duolingo:** Duolingo is a gamified language learning app that makes learning new languages fun and easy. You can choose from a variety of languages, including Spanish, French, German, and Italian. Duolingo is free to use, but you can purchase a subscription for more features.

- **Khan Academy:** Khan Academy is a non-profit organization that provides free educational videos and exercises for various subjects, including math, science, history, and economics. Khan Academy is a great resource for students of all ages.

- **Memrise**: Memrise is a language learning app that uses interactive courses to help you expand your vocabulary and improve your pronunciation. You can choose from a variety of languages, including Spanish, French, German, and Italian. Memrise is free to use, but you can purchase a subscription for more features.

- **Udemy:**Udemy is an online learning platform that offers courses on a wide range of topics, from programming to photography. You can find courses for all levels of experience, from beginner to expert. Udemy courses are typically paid, but you can often find discounts and promotions.

- **TED**: TED is a non-profit organization that shares inspiring talks from experts in various fields. You can find talks on a wide range of topics, from technology to psychology. TED talks are a great way to learn new things and be inspired.

3. Creativity Apps

- **Adobe Lightroom:** Adobe Lightroom is a photo editing app that allows you to edit and enhance your photos with professional tools. You can use it to adjust exposure, contrast, and color, as well as apply filters and effects. Adobe Lightroom is free to use, but you can purchase a subscription for more features.

- **Canva:** Canva is a graphic design app that allows you to create stunning graphics, presentations, and social media posts with easy-to-use templates. You can use it to create invitations, flyers, and even logos.

Canva is free to use, but you can purchase a subscription for more features.

- **GarageBand**: GarageBand is a music creation app that allows you to make music with virtual instruments, loops, and recording capabilities. You can use it to create songs, podcasts, and even ringtones. GarageBand is free to use.

- **Procreate:** Procreate is a digital art app that allows you to sketch, paint, and illustrate with a powerful set of tools. You can use it to create concept art, comics, and even animations. Procreate is a paid app, but it is worth the price for serious artists.

- **VSCO:** VSCO is a photo editing app that allows you to apply artistic filters and editing tools to your photos. You can use it to create a variety of looks, from vintage to modern. VSCO is free to use, but you can purchase a subscription for more features.

4. Entertainment Apps

- **Netflix:** Netflix is a streaming service that allows you to watch movies, TV shows, and documentaries. You can choose from a wide variety of titles, including original Netflix content. Netflix is a paid subscription service.

- **Spotify:** Spotify is a music streaming service that allows you to listen to music and podcasts from a vast library. You can choose

CHAPTER 2: MASTERING YOUR IPHONE APPS

Welcome to the world of iPhone apps, where endless possibilities await you. Your iPhone is not just a phone; it's a powerful tool that can be customized to fit your unique needs and interests. With a vast array of apps available, you can transform your iPhone into a productivity powerhouse, a learning companion, a creative canvas, or an entertainment hub.

Downloading and Installing Apps

Downloading and installing apps on your iPhone is a straightforward process that involves accessing the App Store, finding the desired app, and initiating the download. Here's a step-by-step guide:

1. **Open the App Store:**Locate and tap the App Store icon on your iPhone's Home screen.

2. **Search for the app**: Use the search bar at the top of the App Store to enter the app's name or a relevant keyword. Alternatively, browse through the various categories to discover new apps.

3. **Select the app:** Once you've found the app you want, tap on its icon to view its details page.

4. **Check reviews and ratings:** Before downloading, it's always a good practice to read reviews and ratings from other users to gauge the app's quality and user experience.

5. **Download and install:** If you're satisfied with the app, tap the "Get" or "Buy" button. If the app is free, it will start downloading immediately. If it requires payment, you'll need to confirm your purchase.

6. **Enter your Apple ID password:** If prompted, enter your Apple ID password to proceed with the download.

7. **Wait for the download to complete**: The app will start downloading and installing automatically. The progress will be indicated by a circular progress bar.

8. **Launch the app:** Once the download is complete, the "Get" or "Buy" button will change to an "Open" button. Tap it to launch the app.

9. **Enjoy your new app:** You can now start using the app and explore its features.

Opening and Closing Apps

Opening and closing apps on your iPhone 15 Pro Max is a fundamental part of using your device effectively. Here's a guide on how to perform these actions:

Opening Apps:

1. **Locate the app:** Find the app you want to open on your iPhone's Home screen or App Library.

2. **Tap the app icon:** Simply tap on the app icon to launch the app.

3. **Wait for the app to load:** The app will open and display its interface.

Closing Apps:

To close apps on your iPhone 15 Pro Max, follow these steps:

1. **Access the App Switcher:** Swipe up from the bottom of the screen and pause in the middle to bring up the App Switcher.

2. **Locate the app to close:** Swipe left or right to find the app you want to close.

3. **Swipe up on the app preview**: Swipe up on the app's preview window to close the app.

Remember that closing apps is not always necessary, as iOS efficiently manages background apps. However, closing apps can be helpful if an app is unresponsive or consuming excessive battery power.

Navigating the App Library

The App Library on your iPhone 15 Pro Max is a central repository that organizes all your installed apps into various categories, making it easier to find and access them. Here's how to navigate the App Library:

1. **Accessing the App Library:** Swipe left on your Home screen until you reach the last page. The App Library will appear automatically.

2. **Exploring Categories:** The App Library is divided into several categories, such as Productivity, Social, Creativity, Utilities, and more. Swipe up or down to browse through the categories.

3. **Finding Apps:** Within each category, you'll find app icons arranged in a grid. Scroll through the grid to locate the app you want.

4. **Launching Apps:** Tap on the app icon to launch the app.

5. **Searching for Apps:** If you can't find the app you're looking for, use the search bar at the top of the App Library. Type in the app's name or a related keyword to quickly locate it.

6. **Adding Apps to Home Screen:** If you frequently use an app, you can add it to your Home screen for quicker access. Long press on the app icon in the App Library, and then select "Add to Home Screen".

7. **Managing App Folders:** The App Library also includes app folders, which group similar apps together. Tap on a folder to expand it and view the apps inside.

8. **Hiding App Pages:**If you want to streamline your Home screen, you can hide entire app pages. Long press on an empty area of the Home screen, tap on the page dots at the bottom, and then uncheck the pages you want to hide. Your hidden app pages will still be accessible through the App Library.

The App Library provides a convenient way to manage and access your apps without cluttering your Home screen. By utilizing its features, you can keep your iPhone organized and easily find the apps you need.

Managing Your Apps Effectively

Managing your apps effectively on your iPhone 15 Pro Max is crucial for maintaining a clutter-free, organized device and optimizing your app usage. Here are some tips to help you manage your apps effectively:

1. Organize Your Home Screen:

- **Create folders:**Group similar apps into folders to reduce Home screen clutter. Long press an app icon, drag it over another app, and release to create a folder.

- **Arrange app icons:** Place frequently used apps on the first few Home screen pages for easy access. Long press an app icon and drag it to the desired location.

- **Hide app pages:** If you have many app pages, hide the ones you rarely use to declutter your Home screen. Long press on an empty area of the Home screen, tap the page dots at the bottom, and uncheck the pages you want to hide.

2. Utilize the App Library:

- **Find apps easily:** Use the App Library to quickly locate apps without swiping through multiple Home screen pages. Swipe left to the last Home screen page to access the App Library.

- **Search for apps:** Use the search bar at the top of the App Library to find apps by name or keyword.

- **Add apps to Home Screen:** Long press an app icon in the App Library and select "Add to Home Screen" to place it on your Home screen.

3. Update Apps Regularly:

- **Enable automatic updates:** Set your iPhone to automatically update apps to ensure you have the latest features and security patches. Go to Settings > App Store and enable "App Updates" under Automatic Downloads.

- **Manually check for updates**: Periodically check for app updates manually. Open the App Store, tap your profile icon, and scroll down to see available updates.

4. Uninstall Unused Apps:

- **Free up storage space:** Remove apps you no longer use to free up storage space on your iPhone. Long press an app icon and tap "Remove App" or "Delete App".

- **Reduce clutter:** Uninstalling unused apps keeps your Home screen and App Library organized.

5. Manage App Permissions:

- **Review app permissions:** Regularly review app permissions to ensure they align with your privacy preferences. Go to Settings > Privacy to manage app permissions.

- **Grant permissions selectively:** Only grant permissions to apps that require them for essential functionality.

- **Revoke unnecessary permissions**: Revoke permissions for apps that don't need access to sensitive data or device features.

6. Utilize App Customization Options:

- **Explore app settings**: Many apps offer customization options to personalize your experience. Check the app's settings menu to adjust preferences and features.

- **Enable notifications:** Choose which apps you want to receive notifications from and customize how they appear. Go to Settings > Notifications to manage app notifications.

- **Use widgets:** Add widgets to your Home screen or Today View for quick access to app information and shortcuts. Long press on an empty area of the Home screen and tap the "+" icon to add widgets.

By following these tips, you can effectively manage your apps, keep your iPhone organized, and enhance your overall app experience.

Utilizing Apps with Siri

Siri, the intelligent voice assistant on your iPhone 15 Pro Max, can seamlessly integrate with various apps to enhance your productivity and hands-free control. Here's how to utilize apps with Siri:

1. Launching Apps:

- **Activate Siri:** Say "Hey Siri" or long-press the Side button to activate Siri.

- **Open apps by name:** Say "Open [app name]" to launch a specific app. For example, "Open Spotify" or "Open Camera".

- **Use Siri Suggestions:** Siri can suggest relevant apps based on your usage patterns. Swipe right on the Home screen or Lock screen to access Siri Suggestions.

2. Performing Actions within Apps:

- **Control app features:**Many apps support Siri commands for specific actions. For instance, say "Play my workout playlist" in Spotify or "Set a timer for 10 minutes" in the Clock app.

- **Dictate text:** In apps that accept text input, activate Siri and say "Dictate" to speak instead of typing.

- **Send messages:** Ask Siri to send messages through messaging apps like WhatsApp or iMessage. For example, "Send a WhatsApp message to John saying I'll be there in 15 minutes".

3. Creating Siri Shortcuts:

- **Customize shortcuts:** Create custom Siri shortcuts to automate tasks or combine multiple actions from different apps. Open the Shortcuts app to create and manage shortcuts.

- **Trigger shortcuts with voice:** Assign voice phrases to your shortcuts. Say the phrase to Siri to execute the shortcut.

- **Add shortcuts to Home Screen:** Add shortcuts to your Home screen for quick access. Long press a shortcut in the Shortcuts app and select "Add to Home Screen".

4. Integrating with Siri Suggestions:

- **Enable Siri Suggestions:** Go to Settings > Siri & Search and enable "Suggestions in Search" and "Suggestions on Lock Screen".

- **Access app suggestions:** Swipe right on the Home screen or Lock screen to see Siri Suggestions, including recently used apps and actions.

- **Use suggested shortcuts:** Siri may suggest shortcuts based on your app usage. Tap on a suggested shortcut to execute it.

5. Utilizing Siri for Accessibility:

- **Voice control:** Use Siri to navigate your iPhone and interact with apps hands-free.

- **Dictation:** Dictate text in apps instead of typing, especially helpful for users with motor impairments.

- **VoiceOver assistance:** Siri can assist with VoiceOver, the screen reader for visually impaired users.

By leveraging Siri's integration with apps, you can streamline your tasks, enhance accessibility, and control your iPhone 15 Pro Max more efficiently.

Seamlessly Integrating Apps with Other Devices

Seamless integration of apps across your Apple devices, including your iPhone 15 Pro Max, Mac, iPad, and Apple Watch, can significantly enhance your productivity and user experience. Here's how to achieve seamless integration:

1. Utilize Handoff:

- **Enable Handoff:** On your iPhone, go to Settings > General > AirPlay & Handoff and enable "Handoff".

- **Start a task on one device:** Begin a task in an app on one device, such as composing an email or editing a document.

- **Continue on another device**: Switch to another nearby Apple device and look for the Handoff icon in the app switcher or Dock. Tap the icon to continue the task seamlessly.

2. Leverage Universal Clipboard:

- **Enable Universal Clipboard:** Ensure both devices are signed in with the same Apple ID and have Bluetooth and Wi-Fi turned on.

- **Copy content on one device:** Copy text, images, or other content on one device.

- **Paste on another device:** Switch to another Apple device and paste the copied content into any compatible app.

3. Sync App Data with iCloud:

- **Enable iCloud syncing**: On your iPhone, go to Settings > [Your Name] > iCloud and enable iCloud syncing for the desired apps.

- **Access synced data:** Your app data, such as documents, notes, or game progress, will automatically sync across devices.

4. Utilize Continuity Features:

- **Continuity Camera:** Use your iPhone as a camera for your Mac. On your Mac, open an app that accepts image input, right-click, and select "Import from iPhone or iPad".

- **Instant Hotspot:** Share your iPhone's internet connection with your Mac or iPad without entering a password.

- **Sidecar:** Use your iPad as a secondary display for your Mac. On your Mac, click the AirPlay icon in the menu bar and select your iPad.

- **SMS Relay:** Send and receive SMS messages from your Mac or iPad. On your iPhone, go to Settings > Messages > Text Message Forwarding and enable your Mac or iPad.

5. Third-Party App Integrations:

- Many third-party apps offer cross-device syncing and features. Explore app settings to enable syncing or connect devices.

- Examples include note-taking apps, productivity suites, cloud storage services, and messaging platforms.

By utilizing these integration methods, you can create a cohesive ecosystem where your apps work seamlessly across your Apple devices, boosting productivity and convenience.

CHAPTER 3: TAKING CONTROL OF YOUR DATA

In today's digital age, your personal data is a valuable asset that requires careful management and protection. Your iPhone 15 Pro Max holds a wealth of personal information, from contacts and messages to photos and browsing history. Understanding how to manage and safeguard this data is crucial for maintaining your privacy and security.

1. Understanding Data Privacy:

- **Privacy basics:** Familiarize yourself with the concept of data privacy and why it matters. Learn about the types of data your iPhone collects and how it's used.

- **Apple's privacy stance:** Understand Apple's privacy policies and commitments to protecting user data. Explore features like App Tracking Transparency and privacy labels.

- **Third-party apps and data sharing:** Be aware of how third-party apps collect and use your data. Review app privacy policies and adjust permissions accordingly.

2. Managing App Permissions:

- **Review app permissions:** Regularly check app permissions to ensure they align with your privacy preferences. Go to Settings > Privacy to manage app permissions.

- **Grant permissions selectively**: Only grant permissions to apps that require them for essential functionality.

- **Revoke unnecessary permissions:** Revoke permissions for apps that don't need access to sensitive data or device features.

3. Protecting Your Data with Strong Passwords:

- **Create strong passwords**:Use a combination of upper and lowercase letters, numbers, and symbols for your passwords. Avoid using easily guessable information like birthdays or pet names.

- **Enable two-factor authentication:** Whenever possible, enable two-factor authentication (2FA) for your accounts. This adds an extra layer of security by requiring a code from your phone or another device to log in.

- **Use a password manager:** Consider using a password manager to securely store and manage your passwords. This can help you create strong, unique passwords for each account.

4. Backing Up Your Data:

- **Regular backups:** Regularly back up your iPhone data to iCloud or a computer to prevent data loss in case of device damage or loss.

- **iCloud backup:** Enable iCloud backup to automatically back up your data to Apple's cloud storage. Go to Settings > [Your Name] > iCloud > iCloud Backup.

- **Computer backup:** Connect your iPhone to a computer and use iTunes or Finder to create manual backups.

5. Securing Your iPhone with Biometrics:

- **Face ID or Touch ID:** Set up Face ID or Touch ID for secure authentication. These biometric features use facial recognition or fingerprint scanning to unlock your iPhone and authorize transactions.

- **Strong passcode:** Create a strong passcode as a backup for Face ID or Touch ID. Avoid using easily guessable patterns or numbers.

6. Utilizing Find My iPhone:

- **Enable Find My iPhone:** Enable Find My iPhone to locate, lock, or erase your iPhone remotely if it's lost or stolen. Go to Settings > [Your Name] > Find My.

- **Mark as lost:** If your iPhone is lost, mark it as lost in Find My iPhone to lock it with a passcode and display a custom message.

7. Keeping Your iPhone Updated:

- **Software updates:** Regularly install software updates to ensure your iPhone has the latest security patches and bug fixes. Go to Settings > General > Software Update.

- **App updates:** Enable automatic app updates to keep your apps up to date with the latest security enhancements. Go to Settings > App Store and enable "App Updates" under Automatic Downloads.

By following these guidelines, you can take control of your data, protect your privacy, and ensure your iPhone 15 Pro Max remains a secure and trusted companion in your digital life.

Managing Your Storage Space Efficiently

Managing your iPhone 15 Pro Max's storage space efficiently is crucial for maintaining optimal performance and ensuring you have ample room for your apps, photos, videos, and other data. Here are some effective strategies to optimize your storage:

1. Identify Storage Usage:

- **Check storage overview:** Go to Settings > General > iPhone Storage to see a breakdown of how your storage is being used.

- **Identify storage hogs:**** Identify which apps or data categories are consuming the most storage. This will help you prioritize what to remove or offload.

2. Remove Unused Apps:

- **Uninstall apps:** Uninstall apps you no longer use or need. Long press an app icon and tap "Remove App" or "Delete App".

- **Offload unused apps:** Offload apps to free up storage while keeping their documents and data intact. Go to Settings > General > iPhone Storage and tap "Offload App" next to an app.

3. Manage Photos and Videos:

- **Review and delete:** Regularly review your photos and videos and delete those you don't need or want.

- **Optimize storage:** Enable iCloud Photo Library to store full-resolution photos and videos in iCloud while keeping optimized versions on your iPhone. Go to Settings > Photos and enable "Optimize iPhone Storage".

4. Manage Messages and Attachments:

- **Delete old conversations:** Delete old iMessage and SMS conversations that you no longer need.

- **Review attachments:** Review attachments in messages and delete unnecessary ones, such as large videos or documents.

5. Stream Music and Videos:

- **Streaming services:**Utilize streaming services like Apple Music or Spotify for music and services like Netflix or YouTube for videos instead of storing large media files locally.

- **Download selectively:** If you download media, choose lower quality options to save storage space.

6. Clear Browser Cache:

- **Clear Safari cache:** Regularly clear Safari's cache and website data to free up storage. Go to Settings > Safari > Clear History and Website Data.

- **Manage third-party browser data:** If you use other browsers, check their settings to clear cache and data.

7. Utilize Cloud Storage:

- **iCloud Drive:** Store documents and files in iCloud Drive to access them from any device without taking up local storage.

- **Third-party cloud storage:** Consider using third-party cloud storage services like Dropbox or Google Drive for additional storage options.

By following these strategies, you can effectively manage your iPhone 15 Pro Max's storage space, ensuring you have enough room for the content you need and enjoy a smooth and responsive device experience.

Backing Up Your iPhone for Secure Data Preservation

Backing up your iPhone 15 Pro Max is a crucial step in safeguarding your valuable data, ensuring you have a copy in case of device loss, damage, or software issues. Here's how to create and manage backups:

1. iCloud Backup:

- Enable iCloud Backup: Go to Settings > [Your Name] > iCloud > iCloud Backup. Toggle on "iCloud Backup" and tap "Back Up Now" to initiate a backup.

- Automatic backups: With iCloud Backup enabled, your iPhone will automatically back up to iCloud when connected to

Wi-Fi, locked, and plugged into a power source.

- Backup contents: iCloud Backup includes most of your iPhone's data, such as device settings, app data, messages, photos, and videos.

- iCloud storage: Ensure you have enough iCloud storage to accommodate your backups. You can purchase additional iCloud storage if needed.

2. Computer Backup:

- Connect to computer: Connect your iPhone to a Mac or Windows PC using a Lightning cable.

- iTunes or Finder: On a Mac with macOS Catalina or later, open Finder. On a Mac with macOS Mojave or earlier or a Windows PC, open iTunes.

- Create backup: Select your iPhone in Finder or iTunes and click "Back Up Now" to create a full backup to your computer.

- Backup contents: Computer backups include almost all data on your iPhone, including device settings, app data, messages, photos, and videos.

3. Restoring from Backups:

- iCloud restore: If you need to restore your iPhone from an iCloud backup, go through the initial setup process and choose to restore from an iCloud backup when prompted.

- Computer restore: To restore from a computer backup, connect your iPhone to the computer, open Finder or iTunes, select your iPhone, and click "Restore Backup".

4. Backup Frequency:

- Regular backups: Back up your iPhone regularly to ensure you have the most recent data saved. Daily or weekly backups are recommended.

- Backup before major changes: Back up your iPhone before making significant changes to your device, such as updating iOS or performing a factory reset.

5. Backup Verification:

- Verify iCloud backup: Go to Settings > [Your Name] > iCloud > iCloud Backup to see the date and time of your last successful iCloud backup.

- Verify computer backup: In Finder or iTunes, select your iPhone and check the "Last Backup" date and time.

By regularly backing up your iPhone 15 Pro Max, you can rest assured that your valuable data is protected and can be easily restored if needed.

Restoring Your iPhone to a Previous State

Restoring your iPhone 15 Pro Max to a previous state involves erasing the current data and settings and replacing them with a previously saved backup. This can be useful if you encounter software issues, want to revert to a previous configuration, or need to recover lost data. Here's how to restore from different backup sources:

1. Restoring from iCloud Backup:

- Erase iPhone: Go to Settings > General > Transfer or Reset iPhone > Erase All Content and Settings.

- Follow setup process: After erasing, follow the initial setup process.

- Choose iCloud backup: When prompted, select "Restore from iCloud Backup" and choose the backup you want to restore from.

- Data restoration: Your iPhone will restore data from the chosen iCloud backup, including device settings, app data, messages, photos, and videos.

2. Restoring from Computer Backup:

- Connect to computer: Connect your iPhone to a Mac or Windows PC using a Lightning cable.

- Open Finder or iTunes: On a Mac with macOS Catalina or later, open Finder. On a Mac with macOS Mojave or earlier or a Windows PC, open iTunes.

- Select iPhone: Select your iPhone in Finder or iTunes.

- Click "Restore Backup": Click the "Restore Backup" button and choose the backup you want to restore from.

- Data restoration: Your iPhone will restore data from the selected computer backup, including device settings, app data, messages, photos, and videos.

3. Considerations before Restoring:

- Backup verification: Ensure you have a recent backup available before starting the restore process. Check the date and time of your last backup.

- Data loss: Restoring from a backup will erase all current data on your iPhone. Make sure you don't need any data that has been added since the backup was created.

- Software compatibility: If you're restoring from an older backup, make sure your iPhone is running a compatible version of iOS.

- Network connection: For iCloud restore, ensure a stable Wi-Fi connection is available.

Restoring your iPhone 15 Pro Max to a previous state can help you resolve software issues, revert to a preferred configuration, or recover lost data. Remember to back up your iPhone regularly to have a safety net in case you need to restore your device.

Transferring Data from Another Device

Transferring data from another device to your iPhone 15 Pro Max allows you to seamlessly move your important information, settings, and personal content to your new device. Here are the methods for transferring data from different sources:

Transfer from an Old iPhone:

- Quick Start: During the initial setup of your iPhone 15 Pro Max, choose to transfer data from an old iPhone. Keep both devices close together and follow the on-screen instructions.

- Data transfer: This method transfers most of your data, including settings, contacts, messages, photos, videos, and more.

- Wireless transfer: Quick Start uses a wireless connection to transfer data between devices.

2. Transfer from Android:

- Move to iOS app: Download the Move to iOS app on your Android device from the Google Play Store.

- Data transfer: This app transfers data such as contacts, messages, photos, videos, and calendar events.

- Wireless transfer: Move to iOS uses a wireless connection to transfer data from your Android device to your iPhone.

- Limitations: Some data types, such as app data and settings, may not be fully transferable.

3. Transfer from iCloud Backup:

- Restore from iCloud Backup: During the initial setup of your iPhone 15 Pro Max, choose to restore from an iCloud backup. Sign in with your Apple ID and select the backup you want to restore from.

4. Transfer from Computer Backup:

- Restore from Computer Backup: Connect your iPhone 15 Pro Max to a computer with a Lightning cable. Open Finder (macOS Catalina or later) or iTunes (macOS Mojave or earlier or Windows PC) and select your iPhone. Click "Restore Backup" and choose the backup you want to restore from.

Before transferring data, ensure you have a recent backup of your old device. Also, connect to a stable Wi-Fi network for wireless transfers. Transferring data from another device allows you to quickly set up your iPhone 15 Pro Max with your existing information and content, making the transition seamless and efficient

CHAPTER 4: PERSONALIZING YOUR IPHONE EXPERIENCE

Your iPhone 15 Pro Max is not just a smartphone; it's a versatile tool that can be tailored to fit your unique preferences and style. Personalizing your iPhone experience involves customizing various aspects of the device, from its appearance to its functionality, to create an experience that feels truly your own.

Customizing Your Wallpaper for a Personal Touch

Customizing your wallpaper is a simple yet effective way to personalize your iPhone 15 Pro Max and make it reflect your unique style and preferences. Here's a step-by-step guide on how to change your wallpaper:

1. Choose Your Wallpaper:

- Apple's preloaded wallpapers: Apple provides a variety of preloaded wallpapers to choose from. Go to Settings > Wallpaper > Choose a New Wallpaper to browse the options.

- Your own photos: Use your own photos as wallpaper to add a personal touch. Select a photo from your Photos app and tap the Share button, then choose "Use as Wallpaper".

- Third-party wallpaper apps: Download wallpaper apps from the App Store to access a vast collection of unique and creative wallpapers.

2. Set Your Wallpaper:

- Home Screen or Lock Screen: Decide whether you want to set the wallpaper for your Home Screen, Lock Screen, or both.

- Still or Perspective: Choose between a still wallpaper or a perspective wallpaper, which has a parallax effect when you tilt your iPhone.

- Dark Appearance: If you use Dark Mode, consider selecting a wallpaper that looks good in both light and dark appearances.

3. Customize Further:

- Dark and Light: Set different wallpapers for Dark and Light appearances to match your preferred aesthetic.

- Live wallpapers: Explore live wallpapers that animate when you press and hold on the screen.

- Widgets: Add widgets to your Lock Screen to personalize it further with information like weather, calendar events, or reminders.

By customizing your wallpaper, you can add a touch of personality to your iPhone 15 Pro Max, making it a more visually appealing and enjoyable device to use

Tailoring Sound and Vibration Settings to Your Preferences

Tailoring your iPhone 15 Pro Max's sound and vibration settings allows you to personalize how your device alerts you to calls, messages, notifications, and other events. Here's how to customize these settings:

1.Ringtones and Alert Tones:

- Custom ringtones: Set custom ringtones for calls, messages, and other notifications to personalize your audio alerts. Go to Settings > Sounds & Haptics to choose from preloaded tones or select songs from your music library.

- Vibration patterns: Choose different vibration patterns for different types of notifications, adding a tactile element to your alerts.

2. Notification Settings:

- App-specific notification settings: Configure notification preferences for each app to control how and when they notify you. Go to Settings > Notifications and select an app to adjust its notification settings.

- Notification styles: Choose between banner notifications that appear temporarily at the top of the screen or alert notifications that require action to dismiss.

- Sounds and badges: Enable or disable sounds and badge icons for notifications based on your preferences.

3. Do Not Disturb and Focus Modes:

- Do Not Disturb: Utilize Do Not Disturb mode to silence all calls and notifications except for those from specified contacts or apps. Schedule Do Not Disturb for specific times or enable it manually.

- Focus modes: Set up custom Focus modes to filter notifications and minimize distractions during specific activities, such as work, study, or personal time.

4. Accessibility Features:

- LED flash for alerts: Enable LED flash for alerts to receive visual notifications in addition to sounds and vibrations. Go to Settings > Accessibility > Audio/Visual > LED Flash for Alerts.

- Mono audio: Enable mono audio if you have hearing difficulties in one ear. Go to Settings > Accessibility > Audio/Visual > Mono Audio.

By tailoring your sound and vibration settings, you can personalize how your iPhone 15 Pro Max alerts you, ensuring you stay informed while maintaining control over your device's auditory and tactile feedback

Configuring Control Center for Quick Access

Configuring Control Center on your iPhone 15 Pro Max allows you to customize the quick-access panel for frequently used settings and actions, making it more efficient and tailored to your needs. Here's how to personalize Control Center:

1.Accessing Control Center:

- Swipe down: Swipe down from the top-right corner of the screen to access Control Center.

- Accessibility Shortcut: If you have difficulty swiping, set up the Accessibility

Shortcut to triple-click the Side button to open Control Center.

2. Adding and Removing Controls:

- Customize controls: Go to Settings > Control Center to add or remove controls from Control Center.

- Drag and drop: Tap and hold the three-line icon next to a control and drag it to rearrange its position in Control Center.

3. Additional Controls:

- Expanding controls: Tap and hold a control to expand it for more options. For example, tap and hold the brightness control to access a larger brightness slider.

- Home controls: Long press a control to access additional options. For example, long press the Wi-Fi icon to access nearby Wi-Fi networks.

4. Accessibility Features:

- AssistiveTouch: Enable AssistiveTouch to add a virtual button to your screen for accessing Control Center and other actions.

- Voice Control: Use Voice Control to open Control Center with voice commands.

5. Third-party Apps:

- App controls: Some third-party apps offer Control Center integration. Check app settings to see if Control Center options are available.

By configuring Control Center, you can streamline your iPhone 15 Pro Max experience, making it easier and quicker to access the settings and actions you use most frequently.

Setting Up Focus Modes for Distraction-Free Moments

Setting up Focus modes on your iPhone 15 Pro Max allows you to minimize distractions and enhance your focus during specific activities or times of the day. Here's how to create and manage Focus modes:

1.Creating a Focus Mode:

- Go to Settings > Focus: Choose from pre-defined Focus modes like Work, Personal, or Sleep, or create a custom Focus mode tailored to your needs.

- Customize settings: Name your Focus mode, choose a relevant icon, and select the people and apps allowed to notify you during this mode.

- Home Screen and Lock Screen: Set a custom Home Screen page and dim the Lock Screen to reduce visual distractions.

2. Activating Focus Modes:

- Control Center: Open Control Center and tap the Focus icon to enable a Focus mode.

- Automation: Set up automation to activate Focus modes automatically based on time, location, or app usage.

- Share Focus Status: Allow others to see when you have a Focus mode enabled, so they know you're limiting notifications.

3. Additional Options:

- Focus filters: Enable Focus filters to hide distracting content from specific apps, such as work-related emails or social media feeds.

- Allow time-sensitive notifications: Allow urgent notifications to break through Focus modes for important alerts.

- Status icons: Choose whether to display status icons on the Lock Screen to indicate an active Focus mode.

By setting up Focus modes, you can create distraction-free environments tailored to specific activities, helping you stay focused and productive while minimizing interruptions.

Mastering Siri, Your Voice-Controlled Assistant

Siri, the intelligent voice-controlled assistant on your iPhone 15 Pro Max, can be a powerful tool for enhancing your productivity, staying organized, and accessing information hands-free. Here's how to master Siri and make the most of its capabilities:

1.Activating Siri:

- "Hey Siri": Enable "Hey Siri" in Settings > Siri & Search to activate Siri with your voice. Simply say "Hey Siri" followed by your request.

- Side button or Home button: Press and hold the Side button (iPhone X and later) or Home button (iPhone 8 and earlier) to activate Siri manually.

2. Basic Commands:

- Making calls: Ask Siri to call a specific contact, dial a phone number, or answer an incoming call.

- Sending messages: Instruct Siri to send text messages, iMessages, or emails to your contacts.

- Setting reminders and alarms: Ask Siri to set reminders for tasks or appointments and set alarms for specific times.

- Searching the web: Use Siri to search the internet for information, news, or specific websites.

3. Advanced Tasks:

- Controlling smart home devices: If you have compatible smart home devices, use Siri to control lights, thermostats, and other appliances.

- Translating languages: Ask Siri to translate phrases or words into different languages.

- Playing music: Instruct Siri to play specific songs, albums, or playlists from your music library or streaming services.

- Getting directions: Ask Siri for directions to specific locations, including walking, driving, or public transportation options.

4. Personalizing Siri:

- Voice and language: Change Siri's voice and language in Settings > Siri & Search > Siri Voice.

- Feedback: Provide feedback to Siri by saying "Hey Siri, that wasn't right" or "Hey Siri, that was helpful" to improve its responses.

- Siri Shortcuts: Create Siri Shortcuts to automate complex tasks or combine multiple actions with a simple voice command.

5. Privacy Considerations:

- Review privacy settings: Go to Settings > Siri & Search > Siri & Dictation Privacy to manage how Siri data is used and shared.

- Disable "Hey Siri": If you're concerned about privacy, disable "Hey Siri" to prevent accidental activation.

By mastering Siri, you can streamline your daily tasks, access information quickly, and control your iPhone 15 Pro Max with just your voice, making your device more versatile and hands-free

.

CHAPTER 5: UNLEASHING THE POWER OF YOUR IPHONE CAMERA

Equipped with advanced technology and innovative features, the iPhone 15 Pro Max camera empowers you to capture stunning images and cinematic videos with ease. To unleash its full potential, explore the various modes, settings, and techniques that transform your smartphone into a powerful creative tool.

1.Mastering the Camera App:

- Familiarize yourself with the interface: Understand the layout of the Camera app, including the shutter button, mode selector, and various settings icons.

- Accessing different modes: Swipe left or right to switch between Photo, Video, Portrait, and other available modes.

- Adjusting settings: Tap the arrow icon to access settings like flash, exposure, timer, and filters.

2. Exploring Photo Modes:

- Standard Photo mode: Capture everyday moments with automatic settings and intelligent scene detection.

- Portrait mode: Create professional-looking portraits with blurred backgrounds and enhanced lighting effects.

- Night mode: Capture clear and detailed photos in low-light conditions without using a flash.

- Panorama mode: Capture wide-angle panoramic shots by panning your iPhone across a scene.

3. Experimenting with Video Modes:

- Standard Video mode: Record high-quality videos with smooth motion and stabilization.

- Slo-mo mode: Capture slow-motion videos to highlight action sequences or add dramatic effects.

- Time-lapse mode: Condense long periods of time into short, captivating time-lapses.

- Cinematic mode: Record videos with shallow depth of field and automatic focus transitions for a cinematic effect.

4. Utilizing Advanced Features:
   - Live Photos: Capture Live Photos that record a few seconds of video before and after each photo, adding a touch of motion and context.

- ProRAW format: Shoot in ProRAW format for greater flexibility in editing and enhancing photos.

- ProRes format: Record videos in ProRes format for higher quality and more control over color grading and editing.

- LiDAR scanner: Utilize the LiDAR scanner for enhanced depth perception, enabling features like Night mode portraits and AR experiences.

5. Enhancing Your Photography Skills:

- Composition: Pay attention to framing, balance, and leading lines to create visually appealing compositions.

- Lighting: Utilize natural light or experiment with artificial lighting to enhance the mood and atmosphere of your photos.

- Editing: Use the built-in editing tools or third-party apps to adjust brightness, contrast, saturation, and other aspects of your photos.

6. Sharing Your Creations:

- Social media: Share your photos and videos directly to social media platforms like Instagram, Facebook, or Twitter.

- Cloud storage: Back up your photos and videos to iCloud or other cloud storage services to keep them safe and accessible.

- Printing: Print your favorite photos to create physical keepsakes or personalized gifts.

By mastering the Camera app, exploring different modes, and enhancing your photography skills, you can unleash the full potential of your iPhone 15 Pro Max camera, capturing stunning images and cinematic videos that capture your unique perspective and creativity.

Capturing Stunning Photos and Videos

To capture stunning photos and videos with your iPhone 15 Pro Max, follow these tips and techniques:

1.Composition:

- Rule of thirds: Divide the frame into thirds horizontally and vertically, placing your subject along the lines or at the intersections for a balanced composition.

- Leading lines: Use lines in the scene, such as roads, paths, or architectural elements, to guide the viewer's eye towards the main subject.

- Fill the frame: Get close to your subject to fill the frame, creating a more intimate and impactful image.

2. Lighting:

- Natural light: Utilize natural light whenever possible, as it provides a soft and flattering illumination for most subjects.

- Golden hour: Shoot during the golden hour, the period shortly after sunrise or before sunset, when the light is warm and directional.

- Backlighting: Experiment with backlighting to create dramatic silhouettes or add a glow around your subject.

3. Focus and Exposure:

- Tap to focus: Tap on the screen where you want to focus, ensuring your subject is sharp and in focus.

- Adjust exposure: Swipe up or down on the screen to adjust the exposure, making the image brighter or darker as needed.

- HDR mode: Use HDR mode in challenging lighting conditions to capture details in both bright and dark areas.

4. Creative Modes:

- Portrait mode: Use Portrait mode to create professional-looking portraits with blurred backgrounds and enhanced lighting effects.

- Night mode: Capture clear and detailed photos in low-light conditions without using a flash.

- Panorama mode: Capture wide-angle panoramic shots by panning your iPhone across a scene.

4. Editing and Enhancing:

- Built-in editing tools: Use the built-in editing tools in the Photos app to adjust brightness, contrast, saturation, and other aspects of your photos.

- Third-party apps: Explore third-party editing apps like Adobe Lightroom or VSCO for more advanced editing and creative effects.

- Experiment with filters: Apply filters to enhance the mood or style of your photos, but use them sparingly to avoid over-processing.

By applying these tips and techniques, you can capture stunning photos and videos that showcase your creativity and capture the beauty of the world around you. Remember, practice makes perfect, so keep experimenting and exploring the capabilities of your iPhone 15 Pro Max camera to elevate your mobile photography skills.

Editing Photos to Perfection

To edit your photos to perfection, follow these steps and techniques:

1.Choose Your Editing App:

- Built-in Photos app: The Photos app on your iPhone 15 Pro Max offers basic editing tools for adjusting brightness, contrast, saturation, and other aspects of your photos.

- Third-party apps: For more advanced editing and creative effects, explore third-party apps like Adobe Lightroom, VSCO, Snapseed, or Darkroom.

2. Basic Adjustments:

- Brightness: Adjust the overall brightness of the image to make it brighter or darker.

- Contrast: Increase contrast to make the image more vivid and enhance details, or decrease it for a softer look.

- Saturation: Enhance the intensity of colors by increasing saturation or create a more muted effect by decreasing it.

3. Advanced Adjustments:

- White balance: Correct the color temperature of the image to remove unwanted color casts and make it look more natural.

- Sharpness: Increase sharpness to enhance fine details, but avoid over-sharpening, which can introduce noise.

- Noise reduction: Reduce noise in low-light photos to make them look cleaner and smoother.

4. Creative Enhancements:

- Cropping and straightening: Crop the image to improve composition and remove unwanted elements, and straighten it to correct any tilting.

- Vignettes: Add a subtle vignette to darken the edges of the image and draw attention to the center.

- Selective adjustments: Use selective editing tools to adjust specific areas of the image, such as brightening a subject's face or darkening the background.

5. Applying Filters:

- Enhance mood and style: Apply filters to enhance the mood or style of your photos, but use them sparingly to avoid over-processing.

- Adjust filter intensity: Adjust the intensity of filters to achieve a more natural or dramatic effect.

- Combine filters: Experiment with combining different filters to create unique and personalized looks.

6.Saving and Sharing:

- Non-destructive editing: Edit your photos non-destructively to preserve the original image and make adjustments without losing quality.

- Save as copy: Save your edited photos as copies to keep the originals intact.

- Share your creations: Share your edited photos on social media, cloud storage, or print them to showcase your creativity.

Enhancing Videos with Creative Techniques

To enhance your videos and elevate their storytelling potential, employ these creative techniques:

1.Planning and Shooting:

- Storyboarding: Sketch out a storyboard to visualize your video's narrative and plan shots effectively.

- Variety of shots: Capture a variety of shots, including wide shots, close-ups, and different angles, to maintain visual interest.

- Steady footage: Use a tripod or gimbal to stabilize your footage and create smooth, professional-looking shots.

2. Editing and Post-Production:

- Editing software: Utilize editing software like iMovie, Adobe Premiere Pro, or Final Cut Pro to assemble and edit your video clips.

- Cutting and transitions: Cut between shots to create a dynamic pace and use transitions to connect scenes seamlessly.

- Color grading: Apply color grading to enhance the mood and atmosphere of your video, creating a consistent visual style.

3. Adding Music and Sound Effects:

- Background music: Incorporate background music to set the tone and evoke emotions, ensuring it complements the video's theme.

- Sound effects: Use sound effects to enhance specific actions or create a more immersive experience.

- Audio levels: Adjust audio levels to ensure a balanced mix between music, sound effects, and dialogue.

4. Visual Effects and Titles:

- Text overlays: Add text overlays to introduce titles, captions, or provide additional information.

- Transitions and effects: Use transitions like fades or wipes to move between scenes and apply effects to enhance specific elements.

- Motion graphics: Incorporate motion graphics to create visual interest and enhance storytelling.

5. Sharing and Distribution:

- Social media platforms: Share your videos on social media platforms like YouTube, Vimeo, or TikTok to reach a wider audience.

- Video hosting services: Utilize video hosting services like Vimeo or Wistia to embed videos on websites or share them privately.

Film festivals and competitions: Submit your videos to film festivals or competitions to gain recognition and showcase your talent

Sharing Your Visual Masterpieces with the World

To share your visual masterpieces with the world and showcase your creative talents, consider these effective methods:

1.Social Media Platforms:

- Instagram: Share your photos and videos on Instagram, utilizing hashtags and engaging captions to attract viewers and build a following.

- Facebook: Post your creations on Facebook, connecting with friends and family who can appreciate your work and share it further.

- Twitter: Utilize Twitter to share your visual content with a wider audience, using relevant hashtags and engaging in conversations to gain visibility.

2. Online Portfolios and Galleries:

- Create a website: Build a personal website or portfolio to showcase your work professionally, allowing potential clients or collaborators to discover your talent.

- Online galleries: Utilize online galleries like Behance or DeviantArt to share your creations with a community of artists and designers.

- Embedding videos: Embed your videos on your website or blog using video hosting services like Vimeo or YouTube to showcase your work seamlessly.

3. Photo and Video Sharing Platforms:

- YouTube: Upload your videos to YouTube, the largest video-sharing platform, to reach a global audience and potentially monetize your content.

- Vimeo: Share high-quality videos on Vimeo, known for its creative community and focus on independent filmmakers.

- Flickr: Utilize Flickr to share high-resolution photos with a community of photographers, gaining feedback and exposure for your work.

4. Printing and Physical Displays:

- Photo prints: Print your best photos to create physical keepsakes or personalized gifts, sharing your work in a tangible format.

- Photo books: Create photo books to compile your work into a curated collection, preserving memories and showcasing your photography skills.

- Exhibitions: Participate in local art exhibitions or photography shows to display your work in a physical setting and connect with art enthusiasts.

By utilizing these methods, you can effectively share your visual masterpieces with a wider audience, gain recognition for your talent, and connect with fellow creative individuals. Remember to always respect copyright laws and obtain permission when sharing content that is not your own.

CHAPTER 6: EXPLORING THE WORLD WIDE WEB WITH YOUR IPHONE

Your iPhone 15 Pro Max serves as a powerful tool for navigating the vast expanse of the internet, providing seamless access to information, entertainment, and connection. With its intuitive browser and advanced features, you can explore the World Wide Web with ease and efficiency.

1.Safari: Your Gateway to the Web:

- Default browser: Safari is the default web browser on your iPhone, offering a streamlined interface and seamless integration with Apple's ecosystem.

- Navigating the web: Use the address bar to enter URLs or search terms, and swipe left or right to navigate between open tabs.

- Bookmarks and favorites: Save frequently visited websites as bookmarks for quick access.

2. Enhancing Your Browsing Experience:

- Private browsing: Enable private browsing mode to prevent Safari from storing your browsing history or cookies.

- Reader mode: Use Reader mode to remove distractions and focus on the main content of a webpage.

- Content blockers: Install content blockers to prevent ads and other unwanted elements from cluttering your browsing experience.

3. Search Engines and Information Gathering:

- Google, Bing, DuckDuckGo: Utilize search engines like Google, Bing, or DuckDuckGo to find information on any topic imaginable.

- Refine your searches: Use advanced search operators to refine your searches and get more relevant results.

- Evaluate sources: Critically evaluate the credibility and reliability of online sources before accepting information as accurate.

4. Social Media and Online Communities:

- Connect with friends and family: Stay connected with friends and family through social media platforms like Facebook, Instagram, or Twitter.

- Join online communities: Engage in online communities and forums related to your interests to share knowledge and connect with like-minded individuals.

- Curating your social media experience: Tailor your social media feeds to prioritize meaningful content and minimize negativity.

5. Social Media and Online Communities:

- Connect with friends and family: Stay connected with friends and family through social media platforms like Facebook, Instagram, or Twitter.

- Join online communities: Engage in online communities and forums related to your interests to share knowledge and connect with like-minded individuals.

- Curating your social media experience: Tailor your social media feeds to prioritize meaningful content and minimize negativity.

6. Entertainment and Leisure:

- Streaming services: Access streaming services like Netflix, Hulu, or Spotify to enjoy movies, TV shows, and music on demand.

- Online gaming: Play online games to challenge yourself, compete with others, or simply relax and have fun.

- Exploring new hobbies: Discover new hobbies and interests through online tutorials, forums, and communities.

7. Staying Safe and Secure Online:

- Strong passwords: Use strong, unique passwords for all your online accounts to protect your personal information.

- Beware of phishing scams: Be cautious of emails or messages that ask for personal information or direct you to suspicious websites.

- Public Wi-Fi security: Use a VPN when connecting to public Wi-Fi networks to safeguard your data from potential interception.

With your iPhone 15 Pro Max as your guide, you can embark on a journey through the World Wide Web, unlocking a world of information, entertainment, and connection. Remember to browse responsibly, protect your privacy, and always seek out reliable sources of information.

Connecting to the Internet Seamlessly

To connect your iPhone 15 Pro Max to the internet seamlessly, follow these steps:

1.Wi-Fi Connection:

- Check Wi-Fi availability: Ensure you are within range of a Wi-Fi network. Look for the Wi-Fi symbol in the status bar at the top of your screen.

- Open Wi-Fi settings: Go to Settings > Wi-Fi and make sure Wi-Fi is turned on.

- Select a network: Choose the Wi-Fi network you want to join from the list of available networks. If the network is password-protected, enter the password when prompted.

2. Cellular Data Connection:

- Check cellular data availability: Ensure you have cellular data coverage. Look for the cellular signal strength indicator in the status bar.

- Enable cellular data: Go to Settings > Cellular and make sure Cellular Data is turned on.

- Data usage considerations: Be mindful of your data usage if you have a limited data plan. Consider using Wi-Fi whenever possible to conserve data.

3. Troubleshooting Connection Issues:

- Restart your iPhone: Sometimes, a simple restart can resolve connectivity issues.

- Reset network settings: If the problem persists, try resetting your network settings in Settings > General > Reset > Reset Network Settings.

- Contact your carrier: If you still cannot connect, contact your cellular service provider to check for network outages or account-related issues.

4. Additional Tips:

- Save Wi-Fi networks: Save frequently used Wi-Fi networks to automatically connect when in range.

- Enable Wi-Fi Assist: Enable Wi-Fi Assist in Settings > Cellular to automatically switch to cellular data when Wi-Fi connectivity is poor.

- Monitor data usage: Track your cellular data usage in Settings > Cellular to avoid exceeding your data plan limits.

By following these steps and employing these tips, you can ensure seamless internet connectivity on your iPhone 15 Pro Max, allowing you to access the vast resources of the online world without disruptions.

Navigating the Web with Safari

To navigate the web with Safari on your iPhone 15 Pro Max, follow these steps and utilize these features:

1.Opening Safari:

- Locate the Safari app: Find the Safari app icon on your home screen or in the App Library.

- Launch Safari: Tap the Safari app icon to launch the browser.

2. Basic Navigation:

- Address bar: Enter URLs or search terms in the address bar at the top of the screen.

- Tabs: Swipe left or right to switch between open tabs.

- Back and forward buttons: Tap the back or forward arrows to navigate through your browsing history.

3. Bookmarks and Favorites:

- Saving bookmarks: Tap the share icon and select "Add Bookmark" to save a website as a bookmark.

- Accessing bookmarks: Tap the Bookmarks icon to view your saved bookmarks.

- Favorites bar: Add frequently visited websites to the Favorites bar for quick access.

4. Search and Find:

- Search bar: Use the search bar to find specific words or phrases within a webpage.

- Find on page: Tap the share icon and select "Find on Page" to search for specific text within a webpage.

5. Advanced Features:

- Private browsing: Enable private browsing mode to prevent Safari from storing your browsing history or cookies.

- Reader mode: Use Reader mode to remove distractions and focus on the main content of a webpage.

- Content blockers: Install content blockers to prevent ads and other unwanted elements from cluttering your browsing experience.

6. Sharing and Saving:

- Sharing webpages: Tap the share icon to share a webpage via email, messaging, or social media.

- Saving webpages: Save webpages for offline reading by tapping the share icon and selecting "Add to Reading List."

By mastering these navigation techniques and utilizing Safari's features, you can seamlessly explore the vast expanse of the internet, accessing information, entertainment, and connection with ease

Utilizing Other Web Browsers for Diverse Options

While Safari is the default web browser on your iPhone 15 Pro Max, there are numerous alternative browsers available that offer unique features and customization options. Here are a few popular choices worth considering:

1.Google Chrome: Google Chrome is a widely used browser known for its speed, cross-platform syncing, and extensive extension library.

2.Mozilla Firefox: Mozilla Firefox prioritizes privacy and security, offering features like Enhanced Tracking Protection and a built-in password manager.

3. Microsoft Edge: Microsoft Edge provides seamless integration with Microsoft services, including syncing with your Windows PC and access to Microsoft Office apps.

4.Opera Touch: Opera Touch is designed for one-handed use, featuring a unique swipe-based navigation system and a built-in ad blocker.

5. Brave Browser: Brave Browser focuses on privacy and ad blocking, offering a built-in ad blocker and the option to earn cryptocurrency through its Brave Rewards program.

When choosing a web browser, consider your specific needs and preferences. If you value speed and cross-platform syncing, Chrome might be a good fit. If privacy is your priority, Firefox or Brave Browser could be ideal. For those who use Microsoft services extensively, Edge offers a seamless experience. And if you prefer a unique and gesture-based interface, Opera Touch is worth exploring.

Experiment with different browsers to find the one that suits your browsing style and preferences. Each browser offers distinct advantages and caters to specific needs, so explore their features and discover the one that enhances your online experience.

Searching the Web Efficiently

To search the web efficiently and uncover the information you seek, follow these strategies:

1.Choose the Right Search Engine:

- Google: Google is the most popular search engine, known for its comprehensive index and advanced algorithms.

- Bing: Bing is Microsoft's search engine, offering a similar experience to Google with a focus on visual search and integration with Microsoft services.

- DuckDuckGo: DuckDuckGo prioritizes privacy, not tracking your searches or collecting personal data.

2. Craft Effective Search Terms:

- Specific keywords: Use specific keywords related to your topic to narrow down the results.

- Use quotation marks: Enclose phrases in quotation marks to search for exact matches.

- Exclude words: Use a minus sign (-) before a word to exclude it from the search results.

3. Refine Your Search with Filters:

- Date range: Filter results by date to find recent or older information.

- File type: Specify file types like PDF or DOC to find specific document formats.

- Website filter: Use the "site:" operator followed by a website URL to restrict results to that site.

4. Advanced Search Operators:

- OR: Use OR between keywords to find results that contain either term.

- AND: Use AND between keywords to find results that contain both terms.

- Asterisk (): Use an asterisk as a wildcard to represent any missing word or phrase.

5. Evaluate Sources Critically:

- Check website credibility: Consider the website's domain (.edu, .gov, .org), reputation, and author credentials.

- Cross-check information: Verify information across multiple sources to ensure accuracy.

- Beware of bias: Identify potential biases or agendas that may influence the information presented.

By employing these strategies, you can navigate the vast sea of online information with greater efficiency, uncovering relevant and reliable sources that enhance your knowledge and understanding. Remember to approach online information with a critical eye, evaluating sources carefully and discerning fact from fiction

CHAPTER 7: UTILIZING YOUR
IPHONE'S VERSATILE FEATURES

Your iPhone 15 Pro Max is packed with a
multitude of versatile features that extend
beyond just making calls or sending messages.
These features transform your device into a
powerful tool for productivity, entertainment,
and personal well-being.

1.Productivity Enhancements:

- Calendar and Reminders: Stay organized
  and manage your schedule effectively
  using the built-in Calendar and Reminders
  apps.

- Notes and Voice Memos: Capture ideas,
  create to-do lists, and record important
  information using the Notes and Voice
  Memos apps.

- Focus modes: Minimize distractions and enhance concentration by setting up Focus modes to filter notifications and limit app access.

2. Entertainment and Leisure:

- Music and podcasts: Enjoy your favorite music and podcasts using the Music app or third-party streaming services like Spotify or Apple Music.

- Games and apps: Explore a vast library of games and apps from the App Store, ranging from casual puzzles to immersive adventures.

- Streaming services: Access streaming services like Netflix, Hulu, or Disney+ to watch movies, TV shows, and documentaries on demand.

3. Health and Wellness:

- Health app: Track your daily activity, monitor your sleep patterns, and manage your overall health using the Health app.

- Mindfulness apps: Practice mindfulness and meditation using apps like Calm or Headspace to reduce stress and improve mental well-being.

- Fitness apps: Engage in guided workouts and track your fitness progress using apps like Nike Training Club or Strava.

4. Utility and Convenience:

- Wallet app: Store your credit cards, loyalty cards, and boarding passes digitally for convenient access.

- Maps and navigation: Get directions, explore new places, and find nearby businesses using the Maps app.

- Camera and photo editing: Capture stunning photos and enhance them using the built-in editing tools or third-party apps like Adobe Lightroom or VSCO.

5. Accessibility and Personalization:

- Accessibility features: Customize your iPhone's settings to accommodate visual, auditory, or motor impairments.

- Personalization options: Tailor your iPhone's appearance, sounds, and notifications to suit your preferences.

- Siri and voice commands: Use Siri or voice commands to control your iPhone hands-free, making calls, sending messages, or setting reminders.

By exploring these versatile features, you can transform your iPhone 15 Pro Max into an indispensable companion that enhances your productivity, enriches your leisure time, and promotes your overall well-being.

Making Secure Payments with Apple Pay

To make secure and convenient payments with Apple Pay on your iPhone 15 Pro Max, follow these steps:

1. Set Up Apple Pay:

- Open Wallet app: Locate and open the Wallet app on your iPhone.

- Add a card: Tap the "+" sign and follow the prompts to add your credit or debit card information.

- Verification: Your bank may require verification, which could involve entering a code sent to your phone or calling your bank.

2. Make Payments in Stores:

- Double-click the side button: When ready to pay, double-click the side button on your iPhone.

- Face ID or passcode: Authenticate using Face ID or enter your passcode if prompted.

- Hold near contactless reader: Hold your iPhone near the contactless payment reader until you see "Done" and a checkmark on the screen.

3. Make Payments in Apps and Websites:

- Select Apple Pay at checkout: When checking out in an app or website, choose Apple Pay as your payment method.

- Confirm payment: Confirm your payment details and shipping address, then double-click the side button to authenticate.

Additional Tips:

- Default card: Set your default card in the Wallet app to make it the primary payment option.

- Express Transit: Enable Express Transit to use Apple Pay without authentication for compatible transit systems.

Lost or stolen device: If your iPhone is lost or stolen, you can remotely disable Apple Pay through iCloud or by contacting your bank.

Sharing Files Effortlessly with AirDrop

To share files effortlessly between your iPhone 15 Pro Max and other Apple devices using AirDrop, follow these steps:

1. Enable AirDrop:

- Open Control Center: Swipe down from the top right corner of your iPhone's screen to access Control Center.

- Long press on wireless connections box: Long press on the box containing Wi-Fi and Bluetooth icons to expand it.

- Activate AirDrop: Tap on the AirDrop icon and choose "Contacts Only" or "Everyone" to determine who can see your device.

2. Share Files:

- Open the file you want to share: Locate and open the file, photo, or other content you wish to share using AirDrop.

- Tap the Share icon: Tap the Share icon, which typically resembles an arrow pointing upwards.

- Select AirDrop: Choose the AirDrop option from the sharing menu.

- Choose recipient: Select the device you want to share the file with from the list of available AirDrop recipients.

Additional Tips:

- Ensure Bluetooth and Wi-Fi are on: Both Bluetooth and Wi-Fi need to be turned on for AirDrop to function.

- Proximity matters: Keep the devices within close range for AirDrop to detect them effectively.

- Accepting files: The recipient device needs to have AirDrop enabled and accept the incoming file transfer.

Troubleshooting:

- Restart devices: If AirDrop isn't working, try restarting both devices to refresh their connections.

- Check software updates: Ensure both devices are running the latest software updates to avoid compatibility issues.

- Reset network settings: If problems persist, consider resetting network settings in Settings > General > Reset > Reset Network Settings.

Leveraging iCloud for Seamless Data Management

To leverage iCloud for seamless data management and synchronization across your Apple devices, follow these steps:

1. Set Up iCloud:

Open Settings: Go to Settings on your iPhone 15 Pro Max.

Tap on your name: Tap on your name at the top of the Settings menu.

Select iCloud: Choose the iCloud option from the list of settings.

Sign in with Apple ID: Sign in using your Apple ID and password.

2. Enable iCloud Features:

Choose iCloud services: Select the iCloud services you want to enable, such as Photos, iCloud Drive, Contacts, and more.

iCloud Backup: Turn on iCloud Backup to automatically back up your iPhone's data to iCloud.

Optimize Storage: Consider enabling Optimize Storage to automatically manage your iCloud storage space.

3. Access iCloud Data:

- iCloud.com: Access your iCloud data, including photos, contacts, and documents, through the iCloud.com website.

- iCloud Drive app: Use the iCloud Drive app on your iPhone to manage and access files stored in iCloud.

- Other iCloud-enabled apps: iCloud-enabled apps like Photos, Notes, and Reminders will automatically sync data across your devices.

Additional Tips:

- Manage iCloud storage: Monitor your iCloud storage usage in Settings > iCloud > iCloud Storage.

- Upgrade storage: If needed, upgrade your iCloud storage plan to accommodate more data.

- Family Sharing: Set up Family Sharing to share iCloud storage and purchases with family members.

- Find My iPhone: Enable Find My iPhone to locate, lock, or erase your iPhone remotely if lost or stolen.

CHAPTER 8: TROUBLESHOOTING COMMON IPHONE ISSUES

While your iPhone 15 Pro Max is a sophisticated device, it's not immune to occasional glitches or hiccups. Here's a guide to troubleshooting common issues and restoring your iPhone to its optimal performance.

Addressing Battery-Related Concerns

To address battery-related concerns and optimize your iPhone 15 Pro Max's battery performance, follow these strategies:

1.Optimize Battery Usage:

- Enable Low Power Mode: Activate Low Power Mode in Settings > Battery to reduce non-essential functions and extend battery life.

- Adjust screen brightness: Lower screen brightness to reduce battery consumption.

- Disable background app refresh: Limit background app activity in Settings > General > Background App Refresh to prevent apps from draining battery in the background.

- Turn off unnecessary features: Disable features like Bluetooth, Wi-Fi, or location services when not in use.

2.Monitor Battery Health:

- Check battery health: Go to Settings > Battery > Battery Health to view your battery's maximum capacity and peak performance capability.

- Consider battery replacement: If battery health is significantly degraded, consider replacing the battery through Apple or an authorized service provider.

3.Charging Practices:

- Use genuine chargers: Use only Apple-certified chargers and cables to ensure safe and efficient charging.

- Avoid extreme temperatures: Avoid charging your iPhone in extreme hot or cold environments, as this can damage the battery.

- Optimize charging habits: Charge your iPhone regularly, avoiding deep discharges and overcharging.

4.Troubleshooting Battery Issues:

- Restart your iPhone: A simple restart can sometimes resolve minor battery-related glitches.

- Update iOS: Ensure you have the latest iOS updates installed, as they may address battery-related bugs.

- Calibrate battery: If battery readings seem inaccurate, try calibrating the battery by fully draining and recharging it.

5.Seek Professional Help:

- Contact Apple Support: If battery issues persist despite these measures, contact Apple Support for further diagnosis and potential hardware repairs.

By implementing these strategies and adopting mindful charging practices, you can maximize your iPhone 15 Pro Max's battery performance and minimize battery-related concerns.

Resolving Wi-Fi Connectivity Issues

To resolve Wi-Fi connectivity issues on your iPhone 15 Pro Max and restore seamless internet access, follow these troubleshooting steps:

1.Basic Checks:
- Verify Wi-Fi availability: Ensure you are within range of a functioning Wi-Fi

network. Check for the Wi-Fi symbol in the status bar.

- Check Wi-Fi settings: Go to Settings > Wi-Fi and ensure Wi-Fi is turned on. Select the correct Wi-Fi network and enter the password if prompted.

- Restart your iPhone: A simple restart can often resolve minor connectivity glitches.

2.Advanced Troubleshooting:
- Toggle Airplane Mode: Turn Airplane Mode on and off to refresh network connections.

- Forget and reconnect to Wi-Fi: Tap the "i" icon next to the Wi-Fi network and select "Forget This Network." Then reconnect to the network.

- Reset network settings: If issues persist, go to Settings > General > Reset > Reset

Network Settings. This will erase saved Wi-Fi networks and passwords.

- Update iOS: Check for and install the latest iOS updates, as they may address Wi-Fi-related bugs.

- Router troubleshooting: Restart your Wi-Fi router or modem. If possible, check for firmware updates for your router.

3. External Factors:
- Interference: Move closer to the Wi-Fi router to minimize interference from walls or other electronic devices.

- Network congestion: If many devices are connected to the same Wi-Fi network, it may cause congestion and slow speeds.

- ISP issues: Contact your internet service provider to check for outages or service disruptions in your area.

4. Seek Professional Help:

- Contact Apple Support: If Wi-Fi issues persist despite these measures, contact Apple Support for further diagnosis and potential hardware repairs.

By following these troubleshooting steps and considering external factors, you can effectively resolve Wi-Fi connectivity issues and restore reliable internet access on your iPhone 15 Pro Max.

Tackling Cellular Data Challenges

To tackle cellular data challenges and ensure seamless connectivity on your iPhone 15 Pro Max, follow these troubleshooting steps:

1.Basic Checks:

- Verify cellular data availability: Ensure you are in an area with cellular coverage. Check for the cellular signal strength indicator in the status bar.

- Check cellular data settings: Go to Settings > Cellular and ensure cellular data is turned on.

- Restart your iPhone: A simple restart can often resolve minor connectivity glitches.

2. Advanced Troubleshooting:
   - Toggle Airplane Mode: Turn Airplane Mode on and off to refresh network connections.

   - Check for carrier settings updates: Go to Settings > General > About and check for carrier settings updates.

   - Reset network settings: If issues persist, go to Settings > General > Reset > Reset Network Settings. This will erase saved Wi-Fi networks and passwords.

   - Update iOS: Check for and install the latest iOS updates, as they may address cellular data-related bugs.

3. External Factors:
- Network congestion: Cellular networks can become congested during peak hours or in densely populated areas, affecting data speeds.

- Carrier issues: Contact your cellular service provider to check for outages or service disruptions in your area.

- Physical obstructions: Thick walls, buildings, or underground locations can block cellular signals. Move to an open area for better reception.

4. Seek Professional Help:
- Contact Apple Support: If cellular data issues persist despite these measures, contact Apple Support for further diagnosis and potential hardware repairs.

- Contact your carrier: If the issue seems related to network coverage or service disruptions, contact your cellular service provider for assistance.

By following these troubleshooting steps and considering external factors, you can effectively address cellular data challenges and maintain reliable mobile internet access on your iPhone 15 Pro Max.

Troubleshooting App-Related Problems

To troubleshoot app-related problems on your iPhone 15 Pro Max and restore smooth app functionality, follow these steps:

1. Basic Troubleshooting:

1.Force-quit the app: If an app is unresponsive or frozen, force-quit it by swiping up from the bottom of the screen and holding until the app disappears.

2. Restart your iPhone: A simple restart can often resolve minor app glitches or performance issues.

3. Update the app: Check for and install any available updates for the problematic app. Updates often address bugs and compatibility issues.

2. Advanced Troubleshooting:

4. Check app permissions: Ensure the app has the necessary permissions to access relevant functions, such as location, camera, or microphone. Go to Settings > Privacy and check the app's permissions.

5. Clear app data and cache: Navigate to Settings > General > iPhone Storage. Select the app and tap "Offload App" to clear temporary data without deleting the app itself. If the issue persists, tap "Delete App" to remove the app and its data entirely. Reinstall the app from the App Store.

6. Check for iOS compatibility: Ensure the app is compatible with the latest version of iOS installed on your iPhone. If the app is outdated and no longer supported by the developer, it may not function properly on newer iOS versions.

7. Contact app developer: If the issue persists and seems specific to a particular app, contact the app developer for further assistance. They may be aware of specific bugs or compatibility issues and provide guidance.

3. System-Level Solutions:

8. Update iOS: Check for and install the latest iOS updates, as they may address general app stability and compatibility issues.

9. Reset all settings: If app problems persist across multiple apps, consider resetting all settings in Settings > General > Reset > Reset All Settings. This will revert all settings to their defaults but won't erase your data.

10. Contact Apple Support: If app issues are widespread and affect multiple apps, contact Apple Support for further diagnosis and potential hardware-related problems.

By following these troubleshooting steps, you can effectively address app-related problems on your iPhone 15 Pro Max and restore seamless app functionality

Seeking Additional Support for Complex Issues

When dealing with complex iPhone issues that extend beyond basic troubleshooting steps, seeking additional support from reliable sources is crucial. Here are some options for obtaining expert assistance:

1. Apple Support:

Apple Support is the official support channel provided by Apple, offering a comprehensive range of support options for iPhone users:

- Online Support: Visit Apple's support website (https://support.apple.com/iphone) for a vast collection of troubleshooting guides, FAQs, and community forums.

- Phone Support: Contact Apple Support via phone for personalized assistance from trained technicians.

- In-Person Support: Schedule an appointment at an Apple Store or authorized service provider for hands-on diagnosis and repairs.

2. Online Forums and Communities:

Numerous online forums and communities dedicated to Apple products offer a platform for seeking peer-to-peer support:

- Apple Support Communities: Apple's official online community where users share experiences, offer solutions, and exchange troubleshooting tips.

- MacRumors Forums: A popular forum with a dedicated section for iPhone troubleshooting and discussions.

- iMore Forums: Another active forum where iPhone users share insights and provide assistance to one another.

3. Third-Party Repair Services:

- If hardware-related issues are suspected, consider seeking assistance from reputable third-party repair services:

- iFixit: iFixit provides detailed repair guides, replacement parts, and tools for DIY enthusiasts.

- uBreakiFix: An authorized Apple service provider with nationwide locations offering professional repair services.

- Geek Squad: Best Buy's Geek Squad offers in-store and in-home repair services for various electronic devices, including iPhones.

When seeking additional support, always prioritize official channels like Apple Support and authorized service providers to ensure reliable and certified assistance. Online forums can offer valuable insights, but exercise caution when following unofficial troubleshooting advice.

CHAPTER 9: NAVIGATING THE BUILT-IN APPS

Your iPhone 15 Pro Max comes equipped with a suite of built-in apps designed to enhance your productivity, communication, and entertainment experiences. Here's a guide to navigating these essential apps:

Mastering the Phone App for Seamless Communication

To master the Phone app on your iPhone 15 Pro Max and elevate your communication experience, follow these tips and techniques:

1.Making Calls:

- Recents: Access your recent calls list to quickly redial or return missed calls.

- Favorites: Add frequently contacted individuals to your Favorites list for one-tap dialing.

- Keypad: Manually enter phone numbers using the keypad, ensuring accuracy.

- Contacts: Search and select contacts from your comprehensive contact list.

2. Receiving Calls:

- Answering Calls: Swipe the green answer button to accept an incoming call.

- Rejecting Calls: Swipe the red decline button to reject a call. You can also send a preset text message to the caller explaining why you're unavailable.

- Silence Incoming Calls: Quickly silence an incoming call by pressing the side button or volume buttons.

- Do Not Disturb: Enable Do Not Disturb mode to silence all calls and notifications during specific times or when you need uninterrupted focus.

3. Managing Contacts:

- Adding Contacts: Create new contacts by entering their name, phone number, email address, and other relevant details.

- Editing Contacts: Update contact information as needed to maintain accuracy.

- Assigning Photos: Personalize contacts by adding their photos for easy identification.

- Organizing Groups: Create contact groups to categorize contacts based on relationships, work, or other criteria.

4. Voicemail:

- Visual Voicemail: View a list of your voicemail messages and select specific ones to listen to, without the need to dial into voicemail.

- Transcriptions: Enable voicemail transcriptions to have your voicemail messages automatically converted into text for quick reading.

- Call Back: Directly call back the person who left a voicemail message with a single tap.

- Sharing Voicemails: Share voicemail messages with others via Messages, email, or other sharing options.

Additional Features:

- Call Waiting: Receive notifications of incoming calls while you're already on a call, allowing you to decide whether to answer or decline the new call.

- Caller ID: Identify unknown callers by enabling Caller ID, which displays the caller's name or information if available.

- Call Blocking: Block unwanted or spam callers to prevent them from reaching you.

- Emergency SOS: Quickly access emergency services by pressing the side button and volume button simultaneously.

By mastering these features and techniques, you can transform your iPhone's Phone app into a powerful communication hub, streamlining your calling experience and enhancing your overall connectivity.

Utilizing the Messages App for Instant Messaging

To effectively utilize the Messages app on your iPhone 15 Pro Max for seamless instant messaging, follow these tips and techniques:

1.Sending Messages:

- Individual Messages: Compose text messages to individual contacts by selecting them from your contact list or entering their phone number or email address.

- Group Messages: Create group chats to communicate with multiple people simultaneously. Add participants from your contacts or by entering their phone numbers or email addresses.

- Emojis and GIFs: Enhance your messages with expressive emojis and animated GIFs to convey emotions and add personality to your conversations.

- Attachments: Attach photos, videos, documents, and other files to your messages to share content beyond just text.

2. Receiving Messages:

- Notifications: Receive notifications for new messages, allowing you to quickly view and respond to incoming conversations.

- Read Receipts: Enable read receipts to let others know when you've read their messages.

- Typing Indicators: See when someone is typing a message in a conversation, indicating that a response is forthcoming.

- Mute Conversations: Mute specific conversations to temporarily silence notifications without leaving the chat.

3. Advanced Messaging Features:

- Memoji and Animoji: Create personalized avatars called Memoji or use animated

Animoji characters to add a fun and expressive touch to your messages.

- iMessage Effects: Apply message effects like bubble effects and full-screen animations to add visual flair to your conversations.

- Digital Touch: Send sketches, taps, or heartbeats using Digital Touch to convey emotions and interactions beyond words.

- Location Sharing: Share your real-time location with specific contacts for a predetermined time, making it easier to meet up or coordinate plans.

4. Conversation Management:

- Search: Easily locate specific conversations or messages using the search bar.

- Pinning Conversations: Pin important conversations to the top of your list for quick access.

- Deleting Conversations: Remove unwanted or old conversations to keep your message list organized.

- Message Effects: Apply message effects like bubble effects and full-screen animations to add visual flair to your conversations.

Additional Features:

- SMS/MMS: Send and receive SMS and MMS messages with non-iPhone users.

- Group Naming: Assign custom names and icons to group chats for easier identification.

- Do Not Disturb: Enable Do Not Disturb mode to silence message notifications during specific times or when you need uninterrupted focus.

By mastering these features and techniques, you can transform your iPhone's Messages app into a versatile communication tool, enhancing your instant messaging experience and staying connected with ease.

Conquering Email Management with the Mail App

To conquer email management and achieve inbox mastery with the Mail app on your iPhone 15 Pro Max, follow these strategies and techniques:

1. Account Setup and Organization:
   - Add Email Accounts: Set up multiple email accounts from various providers like Gmail, iCloud, Outlook, and others.

- Customize Mailboxes: Create custom mailboxes to categorize emails based on projects, topics, or other criteria.

- Smart Mailboxes: Utilize Smart Mailboxes to automatically filter emails based on predefined rules, keeping your inbox organized.

2. Composing and Sending Emails:
   - Compose New Emails: Create new emails with ease, adding recipients, subject lines, and email content.

   - Formatting Options: Format your emails using various text styles, font sizes, and colors to enhance readability.

   - Attachments: Attach files, photos, or documents to your emails to share additional content.

- Signatures: Create personalized email signatures with your contact information or a professional tagline.

3. Receiving and Managing Emails:
   - Notifications: Receive notifications for new emails, allowing you to quickly check and respond to important messages.

   - Flagging and Marking as Unread: Flag important emails or mark them as unread to revisit them later.

   - Search and Filters: Easily locate specific emails using the search bar or apply filters based on sender, recipient, or keywords.

   - Swipe Gestures: Use swipe gestures to quickly archive, flag, or delete emails without opening them.

4. Advanced Email Management:

- VIP Lists: Add important contacts to your VIP list to ensure their emails stand out and receive priority notifications.

- Scheduled Send: Schedule emails to be sent at a specific time, ensuring timely delivery without disrupting your workflow.

- Mute Notifications: Mute specific email threads to temporarily silence notifications without missing important conversations.

- Junk Mail Filter: Utilize the Junk Mail filter to automatically move spam or unwanted emails to a separate folder, keeping your inbox clean.

5.Third-Party Email Apps:
- Explore Alternatives: Consider using third-party email apps like Spark, Gmail, or Outlook if they offer features better suited to your needs.

- Sync Across Devices: Ensure your email accounts are synced across all your devices to maintain consistent access and organization.

By implementing these strategies and mastering the Mail app's features, you can effectively manage your email, maintain an organized inbox, and enhance your overall email communication experience

Staying Organized with the Calendar App

To effectively manage your schedule and stay organized with the Calendar app on your iPhone 15 Pro Max, follow these tips and techniques:

1. Creating and Managing Events:

- Add Events: Create new events by specifying the title, date, time, location, and any additional details.

- Set Reminders: Set reminders for events to receive notifications before the event starts, ensuring you don't miss important appointments or deadlines.

- Recurring Events: Create recurring events for regular activities like weekly meetings or monthly appointments.

- Color-Coding: Assign different colors to different types of events for easy visual identification.

2. Navigating and Viewing Events:

- Multiple Calendar Views: Switch between different calendar views, such as day, week, month, or year, to suit your planning needs.

- Search: Easily locate specific events using the search bar by entering keywords or event titles.

- Widgets: Add Calendar widgets to your Home screen for quick access to upcoming events and reminders.

- Sharing Events: Share events with others via email, Messages, or other sharing options to coordinate schedules and appointments.

3. Advanced Calendar Management:

- Multiple Calendars: Create separate calendars for different aspects of your life, such as work, personal, or social events.

- Subscribe to External Calendars: Subscribe to external calendars, such as shared work calendars or public holiday calendars.

- Location-Based Alerts: Set location-based alerts to receive notifications when you're near the location of an upcoming event.

- Travel Time: Add travel time estimates to events to ensure you allocate enough time for transportation.

4. Integration with Other Apps:

- Siri: Use Siri voice commands to create, edit, or check events hands-free.

- Maps: Link events with locations in Maps to get directions and travel time estimates.

- Contacts: Add contacts to events to easily invite them and share event details.

- Third-Party Calendar Apps: Explore alternative calendar apps like Fantastical or Google Calendar if they offer features better suited to your needs.

By implementing these strategies and utilizing the Calendar app's features effectively, you can streamline your scheduling, stay organized, and manage your time efficiently.

Managing Contacts Effectively

To effectively manage your contacts and maintain an organized and accessible address book on your iPhone 15 Pro Max, follow these tips and techniques:

1.Creating and Editing Contacts:

- Add New Contacts: Create new contacts by entering their name, phone number, email address, and other relevant information.

- Complete Profiles: Add additional details to contact profiles, such as company, job title, birthday, address, and social media profiles.

- Assign Photos: Personalize contacts by adding their photos for easy visual identification.

- Edit and Update: Regularly review and update contact information to ensure accuracy.

2.Organizing and Categorizing Contacts:

- Contact Groups: Create contact groups to categorize contacts based on relationships, work, or other criteria.

- Favorites: Add frequently contacted individuals to your Favorites list for quick access.

- Custom Fields: Utilize custom fields to add additional information or categorize contacts based on specific attributes.

- Search and Filters: Easily locate specific contacts using the search bar or apply filters based on name, company, or other criteria.

3. Syncing and Managing Duplicates:

- Cloud Sync: Enable cloud syncing to keep your contacts synchronized across multiple devices and platforms.

- Merge Duplicates: Identify and merge duplicate contacts to maintain a clean and organized address book.

- Import/Export: Import contacts from other sources, such as SIM cards or email accounts, and export contacts for backup or sharing.

Advanced Contact Management:

Linked Contacts: Link multiple contact profiles for the same person to consolidate their information.

Ringtones and Vibration Patterns: Assign custom ringtones and vibration patterns to specific contacts for personalized alerts.

Emergency Contacts: Designate emergency contacts to provide quick access to vital information in case of emergencies.

Third-Party Contact Apps: Explore alternative contact management apps like Covve or CircleBack if they offer features better suited to your needs.

Integration with Other Apps:

Phone: Seamlessly call or message contacts directly from the Contacts app.

Mail: Easily add contacts as recipients when composing emails.

Maps: Quickly get directions to a contact's address using Maps integration.

Social Media: Connect with contacts on social media platforms through integrated links.

By implementing these strategies and utilizing the Contacts app's features effectively, you can maintain a well-organized and accessible address book, enhancing your communication and productivity.

Taking Notes and Capturing Ideas

To effectively take notes and capture ideas on your iPhone 15 Pro Max, utilize the Notes app and follow these tips and techniques:

1.Creating and Organizing Notes:
- New Notes: Create new notes quickly and easily, jotting down thoughts, ideas, or important information.

- Folders and Subfolders: Organize notes into folders and subfolders to categorize them based on projects, topics, or personal preferences.

- Tags: Assign tags to notes for additional categorization and easy retrieval using the search function.

- Pinning Notes: Pin important notes to the top of the list for quick and easy access.

2. Formatting and Enhancing Notes:
   - Text Styles: Format text using various styles, font sizes, and colors to enhance readability and highlight key points.

   - Checklists: Create checklists within notes to track tasks, manage to-dos, and break down complex projects.

   - Tables: Organize information in tables to present data clearly and concisely.

- Attachments: Attach photos, videos, documents, or sketches to notes to provide additional context or visual aids.

3. Advanced Note-Taking Features:
   - Drawing and Sketching: Utilize the drawing tools to create sketches, diagrams, or handwritten notes directly within the app.

   - Scanning Documents: Scan physical documents using the camera and insert them into notes for easy reference and organization.

   - Collaboration: Share notes with others and collaborate in real-time, allowing for joint brainstorming and idea development.

   - Third-party Note-Taking Apps: Explore alternative note-taking apps like Evernote, Bear, or Notion if they offer features better suited to your specific needs.

4. Integration with Other Apps:
- Siri: Use Siri voice commands to create, edit, or search for notes hands-free.

- Reminders: Create reminders from notes to ensure you don't miss important tasks or deadlines.

- Sharing Options: Share notes with others via email, Messages, or other sharing options to collaborate or exchange ideas.

By implementing these strategies and utilizing the Notes app's features effectively, you can capture ideas, organize information, and enhance your note-taking experience.

Setting Reminders for Important Tasks

To effectively set reminders for important tasks and ensure you don't miss deadlines or commitments, utilize the Reminders app on your iPhone 15 Pro Max and follow these tips and techniques:

1. Creating Reminders:
   - New Reminders: Create new reminders by specifying the task, due date, and time.

   - Lists and Sublists: Organize reminders into lists and sublists to categorize them based on projects, topics, or personal preferences.

   - Priorities: Assign priorities to reminders to highlight urgent or important tasks.

   - Location-Based Reminders: Set location-based reminders to receive notifications when you arrive at or leave a specific location.

2. Managing Reminders:
   - Completing Reminders: Mark reminders as completed to track your progress and keep your list organized.

- Snoozing Reminders: Snooze reminders to temporarily postpone them for a later time.

- Recurring Reminders: Create recurring reminders for regular tasks or deadlines.

- Sharing Reminders: Share reminders with others to collaborate on tasks or delegate responsibilities.

3.Advanced Reminder Features:
- Flagged Reminders: Flag important reminders to make them stand out and receive priority notifications.

- Subtasks: Break down complex tasks into smaller subtasks to make them more manageable.

- Attachments: Attach photos, documents, or links to reminders to provide additional context or reference material.

- Third-party Reminder Apps: Explore alternative reminder apps like Todoist or TickTick if they offer features better suited to your specific needs.

4. Integration with Other Apps:
- Siri: Use Siri voice commands to create, edit, or check reminders hands-free.

- Calendar: Sync reminders with your calendar to visualize your schedule and avoid scheduling conflicts.

- Notes: Create reminders from notes to ensure you don't miss important tasks or deadlines.

By implementing these strategies and utilizing the Reminders app's features effectively, you can stay on top of your tasks, meet deadlines, and enhance your overall productivity.

Navigating the World with Maps

To navigate the world with confidence and ease using the Maps app on your iPhone 15 Pro Max, follow these tips and techniques:

1. Finding Places:

- Search: Enter addresses, landmarks, or businesses in the search bar to quickly locate them on the map.

- Browse Map: Explore the map directly by zooming and panning to discover places of interest.

- Categories: Utilize categories like restaurants, attractions, or shopping to find specific types of places nearby.

- Siri: Use Siri voice commands to search for places hands-free.

2. Getting Directions:

- Driving Directions: Get turn-by-turn driving directions with real-time traffic updates to reach your destination efficiently.

- Walking Directions: Obtain detailed walking directions for navigating on foot, including estimated walking times.

- Public Transit Directions: Plan your journey using public transportation, with schedules and route information.

- Alternative Routes: Compare multiple routes to choose the most suitable option based on time, distance, or traffic conditions.

3. Exploring Places:

- Street View: Immerse yourself in a location with 360-degree street-level imagery to get a visual understanding of the surroundings.

- Flyover: Experience a virtual flyover of cities and landmarks to gain a unique perspective.

- Indoor Maps: Navigate indoor spaces like airports, shopping malls, or museums with detailed indoor maps.

- Business Information: View business hours, contact information, reviews, and photos for places of interest.

4. Advanced Navigation Features:
  - Real-time Traffic: Stay informed about current traffic conditions to avoid congestion and plan your route accordingly.

  - Incident Reporting: Report accidents, hazards, or road closures to help other drivers and improve navigation accuracy.

- Offline Maps: Download maps for offline use to access directions and location information even without an internet connection.

- Third-party Navigation Apps: Explore alternative navigation apps like Waze or Google Maps if they offer features better suited to your specific needs.

5. Integration with Other Apps:

- Calendar: Sync Maps with your calendar to automatically get directions to scheduled events.

- Contacts: Easily find directions to a contact's address using Maps integration.

- Ride-sharing Apps: Connect with ride-sharing services like Uber or Lyft directly from Maps to book a ride.

By implementing these strategies and utilizing the Maps app's features effectively, you can navigate the world with confidence, explore new places, and streamline your travel experiences.

Staying Informed with Weather Updates

To stay informed about current and upcoming weather conditions, utilize the built-in Weather app on your iPhone 15 Pro Max and follow these tips and techniques:

1.Location-Based Weather:
- Set Default Location: Set your default location to automatically receive weather updates for your current area.

- Multiple Locations: Add multiple locations to track weather conditions in different cities or regions you care about.

- Location Services: Enable location services to allow the Weather app to automatically detect your current location and provide relevant weather data.

2. Current Conditions and Forecasts:

- Current Conditions: View real-time weather conditions, including temperature, humidity, precipitation, and wind speed.

- Hourly Forecasts: Check hourly forecasts to plan your day and anticipate any weather changes.

- Daily Forecasts: Get an overview of the upcoming week's weather with daily forecasts, including high and low temperatures, precipitation chances, and overall weather patterns.

- Extended Forecasts: View extended forecasts for up to 10 days to plan for future events or travel.

3. Detailed Weather Information:

- Weather Maps: Visualize weather patterns and radar images to track storms, precipitation, and other weather events.

- Air Quality Index: Monitor air quality levels to make informed decisions about outdoor activities.

- UV Index: Check the UV index to protect yourself from harmful sun exposure.

- Severe Weather Alerts: Receive notifications for severe weather alerts, such as tornado warnings or flash flood warnings, to stay safe and prepared.

4. Third-party Weather Apps:
   - Explore Alternatives: Consider using third-party weather apps like AccuWeather or Dark Sky if they offer features better suited to your specific needs.

- Compare Data Sources: Utilize multiple weather apps to compare data sources and get a more comprehensive understanding of weather patterns.

5.Integration with Other Apps:
- Widgets: Add weather widgets to your Home screen for quick access to current conditions and forecasts.

- Siri: Use Siri voice commands to check the weather hands-free.

- Calendar: Sync weather information with your calendar to anticipate weather conditions for upcoming events.

By implementing these strategies and utilizing the Weather app's features effectively, you can stay informed about current and upcoming weather conditions, plan your activities accordingly, and make informed decisions about your daily routines.

Monitoring Your Health and Wellness

To monitor your health and wellness effectively using your iPhone 15 Pro Max, utilize the Health app and follow these tips and techniques:

1.Activity Tracking:
- Track Steps: Use the built-in pedometer to track your daily steps, aiming for a recommended goal of 10,000 steps per day.

- Set Activity Goals: Set personalized goals for various activity metrics, such as steps, distance, or active calories burned.

- Track Workouts: Record and track workouts, including running, cycling, swimming, and various other activities.

- Activity Rings: Monitor your progress towards daily activity goals using the Activity Rings feature.

2. Health Data Collection:
   - Manual Data Entry: Manually enter health data, such as weight, blood pressure, or blood glucose levels, to track trends and monitor changes over time.

   - Connect Health Devices: Pair compatible health devices, such as smartwatches or fitness trackers, to automatically sync health data with the Health app.

   - Health Records: Import medical records from healthcare providers to consolidate your health information in one place.

   - Symptom Tracking: Track symptoms like headaches, fatigue, or digestive issues to identify potential patterns and inform discussions with healthcare providers.

3. Health Insights and Trends:
   - Health Trends: Analyze trends in your health data over time to identify areas of improvement or potential concerns.

- Personalized Insights: Receive personalized insights based on your health data, such as suggestions for increasing activity or improving sleep habits.

- Share Data with Healthcare Providers: Share health data with your healthcare providers to facilitate informed discussions and enhance care management.

4. Wellness and Mindfulness:
  - Sleep Tracking: Monitor your sleep patterns, including sleep duration, quality, and consistency, to identify potential sleep issues.

  - Mindfulness Apps: Utilize mindfulness apps like Calm or Headspace to practice meditation, relaxation techniques, and stress management.

- Breathing Exercises: Engage in guided breathing exercises to reduce stress, improve focus, and promote relaxation.

5. Third-party Health Apps:
   - Explore Alternatives: Consider using third-party health apps like MyFitnessPal or Fitbit if they offer features better suited to your specific needs.

   - Comprehensive Data Collection: Utilize multiple health apps to collect a more comprehensive range of health data.

6. Integration with Other Apps:
   - Apple Watch: Pair your iPhone with an Apple Watch to enhance activity tracking, heart rate monitoring, and overall health data collection.

   - Health Sharing: Share health data with family members or trusted individuals to provide support and encouragement.

By implementing these strategies and utilizing the Health app's features effectively, you can gain valuable insights into your health and wellness, make informed decisions about your lifestyle, and proactively manage your overall well-being.

Managing Your Finances with Wallet

To effectively manage your finances and make informed financial decisions using your iPhone 15 Pro Max, utilize the Wallet app and follow these tips and techniques:

1.Payment Cards and Digital Wallet:
- Add Payment Cards: Add credit cards, debit cards, and prepaid cards to your Wallet for convenient contactless payments using Apple Pay.

- Default Payment Card: Set your default payment card to streamline the payment process when using Apple Pay.

- Security and Privacy: Utilize strong passcodes and biometric authentication to protect your payment information and prevent unauthorized transactions.

- Digital Wallet Integration: Use Apple Pay for in-store, online, and app purchases, as well as for transit fares and other contactless payments.

2. Financial Overview and Tracking:
   - Account Balances: Monitor account balances for your linked bank accounts, credit cards, and other financial institutions.

   - Transaction History: View transaction history for each account to track spending patterns and identify areas for improvement.

   - Budgeting: Set spending limits and create budgets to manage your finances responsibly and avoid overspending.

- Financial Insights: Receive personalized insights based on your spending habits and financial goals to make informed financial decisions.

3. Peer-to-Peer Payments:
   - Apple Cash: Send and receive money instantly with friends and family using Apple Cash, a secure and convenient peer-to-peer payment service.

   - Splitting Bills: Easily split bills with friends or roommates by sending and requesting payments through Apple Cash or other integrated payment apps.

   - Donations and Charity: Donate to charities and non-profit organizations directly through the Wallet app using Apple Pay or linked payment cards.

4. Third-party Financial Apps:

- Explore Alternatives: Consider using third-party financial apps like Mint or Personal Capital if they offer features better suited to your specific needs.

- Consolidated Financial Overview: Utilize multiple financial apps to gain a comprehensive overview of your finances, including investments, loans, and other financial accounts.

5. Integration with Other Apps:
- Banking Apps: Connect your bank accounts to the Wallet app to view account balances, transaction history, and transfer funds.

- Investment Apps: Link your investment accounts to track portfolio performance and manage investments.

By implementing these strategies and utilizing the Wallet app's features effectively, you can gain control over your finances, make informed financial decisions, and achieve your financial goals.

CHAPTER 10: IMMERSING IN THE WORLD OF APPLE MUSIC

Apple Music, a gateway to a vast universe of music, is an integral part of the iPhone experience, offering a seamless way to discover, enjoy, and share music. To fully immerse yourself in this world of melodies and rhythms, follow these tips and techniques:

1.Exploring the Music Library:
- Browse by Genre: Discover music by genre, from Pop and Rock to Classical and Jazz, exploring the diverse tapestry of musical styles.

- New Releases and Top Charts: Stay up-to-date with the latest releases and explore the most popular songs and albums, keeping your finger on the pulse of the music world.

- Curated Playlists: Immerse yourself in expertly curated playlists, tailored to specific moods, activities, or genres, offering a guided musical journey.

- Search for Specific Artists or Songs: Utilize the search bar to find specific artists, songs, or albums, quickly accessing your favorites or discovering new gems.

2. Personalizing Your Music Experience:
   - Create Your Own Playlists: Craft personalized playlists, compiling your favorite songs, artists, or genres, reflecting your unique musical taste.

   - Follow Artists and Friends: Follow your favorite artists to stay updated on their latest releases and connect with friends to share music recommendations.

   - Save Songs and Albums: Save songs and albums to your library for easy access and offline listening, building your personal music collection.

- Customize Your Listening Preferences: Adjust audio settings like equalizer and sound quality to personalize your listening experience.

3. Discovering New Music:
   - Recommendations Based on Your Taste: Explore personalized music recommendations based on your listening history and preferences, uncovering hidden gems that align with your taste.

   - Radio Stations and Genre Stations: Tune into radio stations and genre stations to discover new music based on your favorite genres or artists.

   - Explore Music Videos: Watch music videos from your favorite artists or discover new ones, adding a visual dimension to your musical journey.

4. Sharing Music with Others:
  - Share Playlists: Share your curated playlists with friends and family, spreading the joy of music and introducing them to your musical world.

  - Social Media Integration: Connect your Apple Music account to social media platforms to share your listening activity and discover music shared by friends.

  - Collaborative Playlists: Create collaborative playlists with friends, adding songs together and building a shared musical experience.

5. Enhancing Your Listening Experience:
  - Spatial Audio: Immerse yourself in Spatial Audio, experiencing music with a surround sound effect, creating a more immersive listening experience.

- Lossless Audio: Upgrade to Lossless Audio for higher-quality sound, preserving the original details of the recording for audiophile-grade listening.

- Lyrics View: Follow along with lyrics while listening to songs, deepening your connection to the music and enhancing your understanding of the artist's message.

6. Expanding Your Music Horizons:
- Explore Live Music: Discover upcoming concerts and live music events in your area, expanding your musical experience beyond the digital realm.

- Music News and Interviews: Stay informed about the latest music news, artist interviews, and behind-the-scenes insights, deepening your connection to the music industry.

- Music Podcasts: Dive into music-related podcasts, exploring diverse perspectives on music history, genres, and artist stories.

By utilizing these strategies and exploring the depths of Apple Music, you can transform your iPhone into a personal music haven, enriching your life with melodies, rhythms, and the boundless creativity of the musical world.

Creating Personalized Playlists

To create personalized playlists on your iPhone 15 Pro Max and curate your music experience, follow these steps:

- Open the Music App: Locate and tap the Music app icon on your iPhone's home screen.

- Navigate to Library: Tap the "Library" tab at the bottom of the screen to access your music collection.

- Create a New Playlist: Tap the "+" icon in the top right corner and select "New Playlist."

- Name Your Playlist: Enter a descriptive name for your playlist that reflects its theme, mood, or genre.

- Add Songs: Search for songs or browse your music library to add tracks to your playlist. You can add songs individually or select multiple songs at once.

- Customize Playlist Details: Tap the three dots (...) next to your playlist name to access additional options. Here, you can add a description, customize the artwork, and make the playlist public or private.

- Arrange Songs: Reorder songs by dragging and dropping them into the desired sequence.

- Save and Enjoy: Once you've added and arranged your songs, your playlist is ready to be enjoyed. Tap the "Done" button to save your changes.

Additional Tips:

- Curating for Specific Moods or Activities: Create playlists tailored to specific moods, activities, or occasions, such as workout playlists, relaxing playlists, or party playlists.

- Discovering New Music: Use the "Suggested Songs" feature to add recommended songs that match the overall vibe of your playlist.

- Sharing Playlists: Share your playlists with friends and family by sending them a link or making the playlist public.

By creating personalized playlists, you can curate your music experience, organize your favorite tracks, and discover new music that resonates with your tastes and preferences.

Sharing Music with Friends and Family

To share music with friends and family using your iPhone 15 Pro Max, you can utilize various methods to spread the joy of music and connect with others through shared musical experiences:

1.Share Playlists:

- Sharing Options: Open a playlist you've created and tap the three dots (...) icon. Select "Share" and choose a sharing method, such as Messages, email, or social media.

- Public Playlists: Make a playlist public by tapping the three dots (...) icon and toggling the "Public Playlist" option. Anyone with the link can access and listen to the playlist.

2.Social Media Integration:

- Connect Accounts: Link your Apple Music account to social media platforms like Facebook or Twitter to share your listening activity and discover music shared by friends.

- Share Songs and Albums: Directly share songs or albums from Apple Music to social media platforms, allowing friends to listen to the same music.

3.Collaborative Playlists:

- Create a Collaborative Playlist: Create a new playlist and tap the three dots (...) icon. Select "Make Collaborative" to allow others to add songs to the playlist.

- Sharing Collaborative Playlists: Share the link to the collaborative playlist with friends or family, inviting them to contribute their favorite songs.

4.AirDrop:

- Sharing Songs: Open a song and tap the three dots (...) icon. Select "Share" and choose "AirDrop" to share the song with nearby Apple devices.

- Sharing Playlists: Open a playlist and tap the three dots (...) icon. Select "Share" and choose "AirDrop" to share the playlist with nearby Apple devices.

5.Third-party Music Sharing Apps:

- Utilize Apps: Use third-party music sharing apps like Spotify or SoundCloud to share music with friends who may not use Apple Music.

- Sharing Links: Generate shareable links from these apps to allow friends to listen to the music even if they don't have an account on the specific platform.

By employing these methods, you can share your musical tastes, discover new music through friends' recommendations, and create shared listening experiences that enhance your connection with others.

Integrating Apple Music with Other Devices

To seamlessly integrate your Apple Music experience across multiple devices, including your iPhone 15 Pro Max, follow these steps:

1.Apple Music Subscription: Ensure you have an active Apple Music subscription to access your music library and playlists across all your devices.

2. Apple ID Sign-in: Sign in to all your devices using the same Apple ID that is associated with your Apple Music subscription. This ensures your music library and preferences are synced across devices.

3. iCloud Music Library: Enable iCloud Music Library on each device. This feature stores your music library in iCloud, allowing you to access it from any device with an internet connection.

4. HomePod and HomePod mini: To play Apple Music on your HomePod or HomePod mini, ensure they are connected to the same Wi-Fi network as your iPhone. You can then use Siri voice commands or AirPlay to control music playback.

5. Apple CarPlay: If your car supports Apple CarPlay, connect your iPhone to your car's infotainment system using a USB cable or

wirelessly. Apple Music will then be integrated into your car's entertainment system, allowing you to control music playback from the car's touchscreen or steering wheel controls.

6.Android Devices: If you have an Android device, download the Apple Music app from the Google Play Store and sign in with your Apple ID. Your music library and playlists will then be accessible on your Android device.

7. Web Browser: To access your Apple Music library from a web browser, go to music.apple.com and sign in with your Apple ID. You can then stream music, manage playlists, and explore new music from any web browser.

By following these steps, you can create a seamless Apple Music experience across your iPhone, HomePod, car, Android devices, and web browsers, enjoying your music library wherever you go.

CHAPTER 11: ENTERTAINING YOURSELF WITH APPLE TV+

Streaming TV Shows and Movies on Demand

To stream TV shows and movies on demand using your iPhone 15 Pro Max, you can utilize various streaming services that offer a vast library of content:

1.Apple TV+: Apple's own streaming service, Apple TV+, provides a selection of original TV shows, movies, and documentaries. It requires a subscription, but you can often get a free trial.

- Accessing Apple TV+: Open the Apple TV app on your iPhone and navigate to the Apple TV+ tab.

2.Netflix: A popular streaming service with a wide range of TV shows, movies, and documentaries from various genres and countries. It requires a subscription.

- Accessing Netflix: Download the Netflix app from the App Store and sign in with your subscription credentials.

3. Hulu: Another popular streaming service offering a diverse selection of TV shows, movies, and documentaries, including Hulu Originals. It requires a subscription.

- Accessing Hulu: Download the Hulu app from the App Store and sign in with your subscription credentials.

4. Amazon Prime Video: Included with an Amazon Prime membership, Amazon Prime Video offers a variety of TV shows, movies, and documentaries, including Amazon Originals.

- Accessing Amazon Prime Video: Download the Amazon Prime Video app from the App Store and sign in with your Amazon Prime account.

5. Disney+: A streaming service dedicated to Disney, Pixar, Marvel, Star Wars, and National Geographic content, offering a vast library of family-friendly entertainment. It requires a subscription.

- Accessing Disney+: Download the Disney+ app from the App Store and sign in with your subscription credentials.

6. HBO Max: A streaming service featuring HBO original programming, as well as a selection of TV shows, movies, and documentaries from Warner Bros., DC, and other studios. It requires a subscription.

- Accessing HBO Max: Download the HBO Max app from the App Store and sign in with your subscription credentials.

7. Other Streaming Services: Numerous other streaming services cater to specific genres or interests, such as Crunchyroll for anime, Paramount+ for CBS and Paramount content, and Peacock for NBCUniversal content.

Once you've chosen a streaming service and signed in, you can browse their library, search for specific titles, and start streaming content directly on your iPhone.

Downloading Content for Offline Viewing

To download content for offline viewing on your iPhone 15 Pro Max, follow these general steps:

1.Open the Streaming App: Launch the streaming app from which you want to download content, such as Apple TV+, Netflix, or Hulu.

2. Locate the Content: Find the TV show, movie, or documentary you want to download. You can browse through categories, search for specific titles, or access your Watchlist.

3. Download Option: Check if the content is available for offline download. If so, you'll see a download icon or option.

4. Initiate Download: Tap the download icon or select the download option. The content will start downloading to your iPhone's storage.

5. Monitor Download Progress: You can usually monitor the download progress from the app's download section or the notification panel.

6. Access Downloaded Content: Once the download is complete, you can access the content from the app's download section or your library, even without an internet connection.

Specific steps may vary slightly depending on the streaming app you're using, but the general process remains the same. Ensure you have sufficient storage space on your iPhone to accommodate the downloaded content

Curating Your Watchlist

Curating your Watchlist on streaming services like Apple TV+, Netflix, or Hulu can be an effective way to organize your entertainment options and ensure you never miss out on titles that pique your interest. Here are some tips for effectively curating your Watchlist:

1.Explore Recommendations: Check out personalized recommendations based on your viewing history and preferences. These suggestions can help you discover hidden gems that align with your taste.

2. Browse by Genre: Explore content by genre, focusing on categories that appeal to you. This can help you find titles that match your mood or interests.

3. Read Reviews and Ratings: Consult reviews and ratings from critics and other viewers to gauge the quality and appeal of a title before adding it to your Watchlist.

4. Follow Actors and Directors: Keep track of your favorite actors, directors, or producers and add titles they're involved in to your Watchlist.

This can help you discover new content based on their work.

5. Prioritize Titles: Organize your Watchlist by priority, placing titles you're most excited about at the top. This ensures you don't miss out on the content you're most eager to watch.

6.Remove Unappealing Titles: Regularly review your Watchlist and remove titles that no longer interest you. This keeps your Watchlist relevant and prevents it from becoming overwhelming.

7. Categorize by Mood or Theme: Create subcategories within your Watchlist based on mood, theme, or genre. This can help you find the perfect title for a specific occasion or preference.

8.Share Recommendations with Friends: Exchange Watchlist recommendations with friends and family to discover new titles and expand your entertainment horizons.

9. Explore Editorial Lists: Check out curated lists and editorial picks from experts to uncover hidden gems and get insights into noteworthy titles.

9. Balance Familiarity and Discovery: Balance your Watchlist with a mix of familiar genres, actors, or directors you enjoy and new titles that push your boundaries and introduce you to fresh perspectives.

Sharing Your Favorite Shows and Movies

Sharing your favorite shows and movies with friends and family can enhance your entertainment experience and foster connections through shared interests. Here are some effective methods for sharing your favorites:

1.Share Links: Copy and paste links to specific shows, movies, or documentaries from streaming services and share them directly with friends through messaging apps, social media, or email.

2. Social Media Integration: Connect your streaming service accounts to social media platforms to share your viewing activity, allowing friends to see what you're watching and discover new titles.

3. Recommendations Feature: Use the recommendations feature on streaming services to suggest specific titles to friends, directly sharing your favorites with them.

4. Create Watchlists for Others: Create curated Watchlists on streaming services and share them with friends, providing them with a selection of titles you personally recommend.

5. Start Discussions: Initiate discussions about your favorite shows and movies on social media or in group chats, sparking conversations and sharing your enthusiasm with others.

6. Host Viewing Parties: Organize virtual or in-person viewing parties to watch your favorite

shows or movies together with friends, creating a shared viewing experience.

7. Share Reviews and Ratings: Write reviews and ratings for your favorite titles on streaming platforms or review websites, helping others discover quality content and providing your perspective.

8.Create Social Media Posts: Share creative social media posts about your favorite shows or movies, using images, quotes, or memes to express your appreciation and generate interest among friends.

9. Recommendations Based on Friends' Tastes: Recommend titles based on your friends' tastes and preferences, tailoring your suggestions to their interests and increasing the likelihood they'll enjoy the content.

10. Engage in Fan Communities: Participate in online fan communities or forums dedicated to specific shows or movies, sharing your passion

with fellow fans and exchanging recommendations.

Enjoying Apple TV+ Across Devices

To seamlessly enjoy Apple TV+ content across multiple devices, including your iPhone 15 Pro Max, follow these steps:

1.Apple TV+ Subscription: Ensure you have an active Apple TV+ subscription to access its content on all your devices.

2. Apple ID Sign-in: Sign in to all your devices using the same Apple ID that is associated with your Apple TV+ subscription. This ensures your viewing progress and preferences are synced across devices.

3. Apple TV App: Download and install the Apple TV app on all your devices, including your iPhone, iPad, Mac, Apple TV, and compatible smart TVs.

4. Content Syncing: Enable content syncing in the Apple TV app settings to ensure your Watchlist, viewing history, and recommendations are consistent across devices.

5. AirPlay and Screen Mirroring: Utilize AirPlay or screen mirroring to cast Apple TV+ content from your iPhone to a larger screen, such as an Apple TV, smart TV, or projector.

6. HomePod and HomePod mini: If you have a HomePod or HomePod mini, you can ask Siri to play Apple TV+ content on the speaker.

7. Web Browser: To access Apple TV+ from a web browser, go to tv.apple.com and sign in with your Apple ID. You can then stream content from any web browser.

By following these steps, you can create a seamless Apple TV+ experience across your iPhone, iPad, Mac, Apple TV, smart TVs, and web browsers, enjoying your favorite shows and movies wherever you go.

CHAPTER 12: CONNECTING WITH IMESSAGE AND FACETIME

Chapter 12 of the iPhone 15 Pro Max User Guide focuses on two of Apple's most popular communication tools: iMessage and FaceTime. These integrated services allow iPhone users to seamlessly connect with friends, family, and colleagues through text messages, multimedia messages, and video calls.

iMessage: iMessage is Apple's proprietary messaging service that offers a rich and interactive messaging experience. With iMessage, you can send and receive text messages, photos, videos, voice messages, and location information. iMessage also supports group messaging, allowing you to communicate with multiple people simultaneously.

FaceTime: FaceTime is Apple's video calling service that enables face-to-face conversations with other iPhone, iPad, or Mac users. FaceTime offers high-quality video and audio, making it an ideal tool for staying connected with loved ones or conducting virtual meetings.

Sending and Receiving Messages Seamlessly

Sending and receiving messages seamlessly is crucial for effective communication, whether for personal or professional purposes. To ensure a smooth and uninterrupted messaging experience, consider these essential factors:

1.Reliable Messaging Platform: Choose a messaging platform that is widely used, compatible with your devices, and known for its reliability. Popular options include WhatsApp, iMessage, Telegram, and Signal.

2. Strong Internet Connection: A stable internet connection is vital for real-time message delivery and notifications. If you're experiencing connectivity issues, switch to a Wi-Fi network or find a location with better cellular reception.

3. Enable Notifications: Ensure notifications are enabled for your messaging app to receive alerts promptly. Customize notification settings to suit your preferences, using specific sounds or vibration patterns for different contacts or groups.

4. Organize Messages: Keep your messages organized by using folders, labels, or archiving features. This will help you track important conversations and easily find specific messages when needed.

5. Clear and Concise Language: Use clear and concise language when composing messages to avoid misunderstandings. Be mindful of the tone and context to ensure your messages are interpreted as intended.

6. Proofread Before Sending: Proofread messages before hitting send to avoid typos and grammatical errors, making your communication more professional and polished.

7. Respond Promptly: Try to respond to messages in a timely manner, especially if they require immediate attention. If you need more time, acknowledge the message and let the sender know when you can provide a more detailed response.

8. Respect Others' Time: Be mindful of others' time zones and schedules when sending messages. Avoid sending messages late at night or early in the morning unless it's urgent.

9. Use Multimedia Sparingly: While images, videos, and voice messages can enhance communication, use them sparingly to avoid overwhelming the recipient or consuming excessive data.

10. Embrace Emojis and GIFs: Emojis and GIFs can add personality and emotion to your messages, but use them appropriately and avoid overdoing it.

By following these tips, you can ensure a seamless, efficient, and enjoyable messaging experience. Effective communication is essential for building strong relationships and achieving success in both personal and professional endeavors

Making and Receiving Video Calls

To ensure a seamless and efficient messaging experience, consider these essential factors:

1.Choose a Reliable Messaging Platform: Select a messaging platform that is widely used, compatible with your devices, and known for its reliability. Popular options include WhatsApp, iMessage, Telegram, and Signal.

2 Maintain a Strong Internet Connection: A stable internet connection is vital for real-time message delivery and notifications. If you're experiencing connectivity issues, switch to a Wi-Fi network or find a location with better cellular reception.

3. Enable and Customize Notifications: Ensure notifications are enabled for your messaging app to receive alerts promptly. Customize notification settings to suit your preferences, using specific sounds or vibration patterns for different contacts or groups.

4. Organize Your Messages: Keep your messages organized by using folders, labels, or archiving features. This will help you track important conversations and easily find specific messages when needed.

5. Communicate Clearly and Concisely: Use clear and concise language when composing messages to avoid misunderstandings. Be mindful of the tone and context to ensure your messages are interpreted as intended.

6. Proofread Before Sending: Proofread messages before hitting send to avoid typos and grammatical errors, making your communication more professional and polished.

7. Respond Promptly: Try to respond to messages in a timely manner, especially if they require immediate attention. If you need more time, acknowledge the message and let the sender know when you can provide a more detailed response.

8. Respect Others' Time Zones and Schedules: Be mindful of others' time zones and schedules when sending messages. Avoid sending messages late at night or early in the morning unless it's urgent.

9. Use Multimedia Sparingly: While images, videos, and voice messages can enhance communication, use them sparingly to avoid overwhelming the recipient or consuming excessive data.

10. Embrace Emojis and GIFs Appropriately: Emojis and GIFs can add personality and emotion to your messages, but use them appropriately and avoid overdoing it.

By following these tips, you can ensure a seamless, efficient, and enjoyable messaging experience. Effective communication is essential for building strong relationships and achieving success in both personal and professional endeavors

Enhancing Communication with iMessage Effects

iMessage effects are a fun and engaging way to enhance your communication and add personality to your messages. They can help convey emotions, emphasize certain words or phrases, and create a more dynamic and interactive messaging experience. Here are some ways to effectively use iMessage effects:

1.Express Emotions: Use iMessage effects to convey emotions and add a personal touch to your messages. For instance, use the "Slam" effect to express excitement or the "Gentle" effect for a more delicate touch.

2. Emphasize Key Points: Highlight important words or phrases by applying iMessage effects. For example, use the "Loud" effect to draw attention to a critical message or the "Spotlight" effect to emphasize a specific word.

3.Celebrate Occasions: Mark special occasions with iMessage effects that match the mood. Use the "Happy Birthday" effect for birthday greetings or the "Congratulations" effect for celebratory messages.

4 Add Playfulness: Infuse humor and lightheartedness into your conversations with playful iMessage effects. Use the "Echo" effect for a humorous repetition or the "Lasers" effect for a fun and energetic touch.

5.Personalize Messages: Create personalized effects using handwritten messages or drawings. This adds a unique and creative touch to your communication.

6. Use Sparingly: While iMessage effects can enhance communication, use them judiciously to avoid overwhelming the recipient or distracting from the message's content.

7.Consider Context: Be mindful of the context and tone of the conversation when using iMessage effects. Ensure the effects align with the overall message and don't misinterpret the intended meaning.

8. Know Your Audience: Consider the recipient's preferences and familiarity with iMessage effects. Use effects that resonate with their style and avoid overdoing it.

8.Combine with Emojis and GIFs: Complement iMessage effects with emojis and GIFs to further enhance the visual appeal and emotional expression of your messages.

9. Experiment and Have Fun: Explore the variety of iMessage effects available and

experiment with different combinations to find what works best for your communication style.

By using iMessage effects thoughtfully and creatively, you can add a spark of personality to your messages, make your conversations more engaging, and strengthen your connections with others.

Adding Fun to Conversations with FaceTime Effects

FaceTime effects are a delightful way to add a touch of fun and creativity to your video calls, making your conversations more engaging and memorable. Here are some tips for using FaceTime effects effectively:

1.Enhance Emotional Expression: Use FaceTime effects to visually convey your emotions and add personality to your interactions. For instance, use the "Hearts" effect to express affection or the "Confetti" effect to celebrate a special occasion.

2.Create a Playful Atmosphere: Infuse humor and lightheartedness into your calls with fun FaceTime effects. Use the "Memoji" effect to transform into a personalized avatar or the "Animoji" effect to mimic your facial expressions with animal characters.

3.Personalize the Experience: Utilize FaceTime effects to create a unique and personalized experience for your calls. Use the "Stickers" effect to add themed graphics or the "Shapes" effect to draw attention to specific areas of the screen.

4.Set the Mood: Choose FaceTime effects that match the tone and context of your conversation. Use the "Studio Light" effect for a professional setting or the "Stage Light" effect for a dramatic presentation.

5.Use Sparingly: While FaceTime effects can enhance your calls, use them judiciously to avoid overwhelming the participants or distracting from the conversation's flow.

6.Consider the Audience: Be mindful of the preferences and familiarity of your call participants with FaceTime effects. Use effects that resonate with their style and avoid overdoing it.

7.Combine with Backgrounds: Complement FaceTime effects with virtual backgrounds to create immersive and visually appealing settings for your calls.

8.Experiment and Have Fun: Explore the variety of FaceTime effects available and experiment with different combinations to find what works best for your communication style.

9.Respect Others' Preferences: If someone seems uncomfortable with FaceTime effects, be respectful and disable them or switch to a more subtle effect.

10.Focus on the Conversation: While FaceTime effects can add fun, remember that the primary purpose of the call is to connect and communicate with others.

By using FaceTime effects thoughtfully and creatively, you can enhance your video calls, make them more engaging, and strengthen your connections with others.

Utilizing iMessage and FaceTime Across Devices

Seamless integration of iMessage and FaceTime across Apple devices is a hallmark of the Apple ecosystem. Here's how to utilize these services seamlessly across your devices:

1.Sign in with Apple ID: Ensure you're signed in to all your Apple devices with the same Apple ID. This enables iMessage and FaceTime to sync messages and call history across devices.

2.Enable Continuity: On each device, go to Settings > General > Continuity and enable

Handoff, which allows you to start a message or call on one device and continue it on another.

3.Set Default Numbers/Emails: In Settings > Messages and Settings > FaceTime, ensure the correct phone number and email address are set for sending and receiving messages and calls.

4.Enable iMessage and FaceTime: On each device, go to Settings > Messages and Settings > FaceTime and enable iMessage and FaceTime respectively.

5.Sync Messages: In Settings > Messages, enable "iCloud Messages" to sync your message history across devices.

6.Use Messages App: Open the Messages app on any device to send and receive iMessages. Messages sync across devices, so you can pick up conversations from any device.

7.Use FaceTime App: Open the FaceTime app on any device to initiate or receive FaceTime calls. Call history syncs across devices, so you can easily continue conversations.

8.Handoff Between Devices: Start a message or call on one device, and a Handoff icon will appear on other nearby devices. Tap the icon to seamlessly continue the conversation on the new device.

9.Group Conversations: Engage in group iMessage chats or FaceTime calls with multiple participants. Conversations sync across devices, so you won't miss a beat.

10.Share Content: Share photos, videos, links, and other content through iMessage. Shared content is accessible across devices, facilitating collaboration.

By following these steps, you can enjoy the seamless integration of iMessage and FaceTime across your Apple devices, ensuring you stay connected and never miss a message or call.

CHAPTER 13: ELEVATE YOUR GAMING EXPERIENCE

Chapter 13 of the iPhone 15 Pro Max User Guide delves into the world of mobile gaming, providing insights and tips on how to elevate your gaming experience on your iPhone. With its powerful A17 Bionic chip, stunning Super Retina XDR display, and immersive audio capabilities, the iPhone 15 Pro Max is a formidable gaming device.

Discovering a World of Immersive Games

Discovering a world of immersive games on your iPhone 15 Pro Max opens up a realm of captivating experiences that transport you to new worlds, engage your senses, and challenge your skills. Here's how to embark on this exciting journey:

1.Explore Genres: The App Store offers a diverse range of game genres, from action-packed adventures to mind-bending puzzles. Delve into genres that pique your interest, whether it's role-playing, strategy, simulation, or casual games.

2. Read Reviews and Ratings: Before downloading a game, check its reviews and ratings to get insights from other players. This helps you gauge the game's quality, gameplay, and overall experience.

3. Try Free-to-Play Games: Many games offer a free-to-play option, allowing you to experience the game without upfront costs. This is a great way to test out a game before deciding to purchase additional content or upgrades.

4. Seek Recommendations: Ask friends, family, or online communities for game recommendations. They might have hidden gems or personal favorites that align with your preferences.

5. Browse Curated Lists: Gaming websites and blogs often create curated lists of top games in

various genres. These lists can introduce you to critically acclaimed titles or hidden indie gems.

6. Follow Gaming Influencers: Follow gaming influencers on social media or video platforms to discover new games and get insights into their gameplay and features.

7. Attend Gaming Events: Attend gaming conventions or online events to discover upcoming games, watch trailers, and interact with developers.

8. Explore AR and VR Games: Immerse yourself in augmented reality (AR) and virtual reality (VR) games that blend virtual elements with the real world or transport you to entirely new environments.

9.Venture Beyond Mainstream: Look beyond popular titles and explore indie games that offer unique concepts, innovative mechanics, and fresh storytelling.

10. Experiment with Different Styles: Don't limit yourself to familiar genres; try games from different styles, such as narrative-driven adventures, artistic puzzle games, or rhythm-based challenges.

By embracing these tips and venturing into the vast world of mobile gaming, you'll discover a treasure trove of immersive experiences that will captivate your imagination and provide countless hours of entertainment.

Recording Your Gameplay for Sharing

Recording your gameplay on the iPhone 15 Pro Max allows you to capture your epic moments, showcase your skills, and share your gaming experiences with others. Here's how to record and share your gameplay:

1.Native Screen Recording: The iPhone has a built-in screen recording feature. To enable it, go to Settings > Control Center, tap "Customize Controls," and add "Screen Recording." Then, swipe down from the top-right corner and tap the record button.

2.Third-Party Apps: Numerous third-party apps offer advanced recording features, such as overlays, commentary, and editing tools. Popular options include Record It!, DU Recorder, and Mobizen Screen Recorder.

3.External Capture Cards: For high-quality recordings, consider using an external capture card that connects your iPhone to a computer. This allows you to capture gameplay directly from the phone's output.

4.Optimize Recording Settings: Adjust the recording settings to match your preferences, such as resolution, frame rate, and audio source. Consider using a higher resolution for detailed gameplay and a lower resolution for longer recordings.

5.Plan Your Recording: Before hitting record, plan your gameplay session, considering what you want to showcase and how to make it engaging for viewers. Practice the game beforehand to ensure smooth execution.

6.Provide Commentary: Add commentary during or after recording to explain your strategies, provide insights, and engage viewers. Use a clear and enthusiastic voice, and avoid excessive background noise.

7.Edit and Enhance: Edit your recording to remove unnecessary parts, add transitions, and incorporate visual or audio effects. Use editing software like iMovie or LumaFusion to polish your video.

8.Share on Platforms: Upload your gameplay videos to video-sharing platforms like YouTube or Twitch. Optimize titles, descriptions, and tags to make your videos discoverable.

9.Promote on Social Media: Share your gameplay videos on social media platforms like Facebook, Twitter, or Instagram. Engage with viewers, respond to comments, and promote your content.

10.Join Gaming Communities: Share your gameplay videos in gaming forums, subreddits, or Discord servers. Engage with other gamers, exchange feedback, and build a following.

By following these tips, you can effectively record, enhance, and share your gameplay experiences, showcasing your skills, entertaining others, and potentially building a community around your gaming content

Sharing Your Gaming Achievements

Sharing your gaming achievements is a way to celebrate your accomplishments, connect with fellow gamers, and showcase your dedication to your favorite games. Here are some effective ways to share your gaming achievements:

1.Game Center: Apple's Game Center platform allows you to track and share achievements with friends. Connect with your friends on Game Center to compare achievements and compete for leaderboards.

2.Social Media Platforms: Share your achievements on social media platforms like Facebook, Twitter, or Instagram. Use relevant hashtags to reach a wider audience and engage with other gamers.

3.Gaming Communities: Join online gaming communities, forums, or subreddits dedicated to specific games or genres. Share your achievements with fellow enthusiasts and discuss strategies or tips.

4.Screenshots and Videos: Capture screenshots or record videos of your achievements to provide visual proof of your accomplishments. Share these captures on social media or gaming platforms.

5.Create Achievement Montages: Edit together a montage of your most impressive achievements, showcasing your skills and dedication. Share the montage on video platforms like YouTube or Twitch.

6.Write Achievement Guides: Share your knowledge and expertise by writing guides on how to unlock specific achievements. Publish these guides on gaming websites or blogs.

7.Host Achievement Challenges: Organize online events or challenges focused on specific achievements. Invite other gamers to participate and share their progress.

8.Celebrate Milestones: Share your progress as you reach significant milestones, such as completing a game or unlocking a rare achievement. Encourage others to share their milestones as well.

9.Showcase Your Trophy Collection: If the game has a trophy or achievement gallery, take a screenshot or video of your collection to showcase your overall progress.

10.Be Respectful and Humble: When sharing achievements, be mindful of others' progress and avoid bragging or belittling others' accomplishments. Celebrate your achievements while encouraging others.

By following these tips and engaging with the gaming community, you can share your gaming achievements in a way that fosters camaraderie, inspires others, and enhances your overall gaming experience.

Enhancing Your Gaming with Accessories

1.Enhancing your gaming experience on the iPhone 15 Pro Max with accessories can elevate your gameplay, improve comfort, and provide a more immersive experience. Here are some essential accessories to consider:

2.External Controllers: For better control and precision, consider using an external controller like the Backbone One or the Razer Kishi. These controllers provide a console-like experience and enhance gameplay for various genres.

3.High-Quality Headphones: Immerse yourself in the game's audio with high-quality headphones or earphones. Choose noise-canceling models for undisturbed gaming or earbuds for portability.

4.Protective Case: Protect your iPhone from accidental drops or scratches during intense gaming sessions with a sturdy protective case. Choose a case that offers grip and doesn't interfere with gameplay.

5.Portable Power Bank: Ensure your gaming sessions aren't cut short by a drained battery. Carry a portable power bank to keep your iPhone charged while on the go or during extended gaming sessions.

5.Gaming Grip: Enhance your grip and comfort during extended gaming sessions with a dedicated gaming grip. These accessories attach to the back of your iPhone and provide a more ergonomic hold.

6.Cooling Fan: Prevent overheating during demanding games by using a cooling fan attachment for your iPhone. These fans help dissipate heat and maintain optimal performance.

7.Wireless Charging Stand: Keep your iPhone charged and ready for gaming with a wireless charging stand. Choose a stand that allows you to view notifications or use your iPhone hands-free while it charges.

8.Screen Protector: Protect your iPhone's display from scratches and fingerprints with a tempered glass screen protector. Choose a high-quality protector that doesn't affect touch sensitivity or screen clarity.

9.Gaming Trigger Buttons: For games that require quick reflexes, consider using gaming trigger buttons that attach to the top of your iPhone. These buttons provide tactile feedback and faster response times.

10.Gaming Stand: Elevate your iPhone to a comfortable viewing angle with a gaming stand. This accessory is particularly useful for strategy games or turn-based RPGs.

By incorporating these accessories into your gaming setup, you can enhance your iPhone 15 Pro Max's gaming capabilities, improve comfort during extended sessions, and elevate your overall gaming experience.

CHAPTER 14: ENABLING ACCESSIBILITY FEATURES

This chapter focuses on the comprehensive accessibility features that make the device more inclusive and adaptable for users with various needs and preferences. These features aim to remove barriers and ensure everyone can enjoy the full functionality of the iPhone.

Utilizing VoiceOver for Enhanced Accessibility

VoiceOver is a powerful accessibility feature on the iPhone 15 Pro Max that enables users with visual impairments to navigate and interact with the device effectively. It provides a comprehensive screen reader experience, narrating on-screen elements, providing audio cues, and enabling interaction using gestures and voice commands.

To enable VoiceOver, go to Settings > Accessibility > VoiceOver and toggle the switch to "On." Once activated, VoiceOver will start narrating on-screen elements as you move your finger around the screen.

VoiceOver Gestures:

- Single Tap: Select an item or activate a control.

- Double Tap: Perform the default action for the selected item, such as opening an app or submitting a form.

- Triple Tap: Scroll down a page or list.

- Flick Left or Right: Move to the previous or next item.

- Flick Up or Down: Move to the previous or next line of text.

- Two-Finger Tap: Stop VoiceOver from speaking.

- Three-Finger Tap: Speak the current item's description.

VoiceOver Commands:

- "VoiceOver, help": Access a list of VoiceOver commands.

- "VoiceOver, speak": Read the current item aloud.

- "VoiceOver, select": Select the current item.

- "VoiceOver, next item": Move to the next item.

- "VoiceOver, previous item": Move to the previous item.

- "VoiceOver, rotor": Access the rotor to change the navigation method, such as by headings, links, or landmarks.

VoiceOver Settings:

- Voice: Choose from various voice options and adjust the speaking rate.

- Verbosity: Set the level of detail VoiceOver provides when describing items.

- Braille: Connect a refreshable braille display for tactile feedback.

- Audio Cues: Enable sound effects to indicate actions or provide feedback.

By mastering VoiceOver gestures and commands, users with visual impairments can effectively navigate the iPhone, access various features, and enjoy a more inclusive and accessible mobile experience.

Magnifying Screen Content with Zoom

The Zoom feature on the iPhone 15 Pro Max magnifies the entire screen or a specific area, making text and details easier to see for users with visual impairments or those who need enlarged content.

To enable Zoom, go to Settings > Accessibility > Zoom and toggle the switch to "On." Once activated, you can use the following gestures to control Zoom:

- Double-tap with three fingers: Zoom in or out.

- Drag three fingers: Pan around the magnified screen.

- Triple-tap with three fingers: Toggle between full-screen and windowed zoom.

Additionally, you can customize Zoom settings to suit your preferences:

- Zoom Region: Choose between "Full Screen Zoom" or "Window Zoom."

- Zoom Filter: Select a filter to enhance contrast and visibility.

- Zoom Controller: Choose a method for controlling Zoom, such as gestures or an on-screen controller.

- Maximum Zoom Level: Set the maximum magnification level.

- Follow Focus: Enable this option to automatically follow the text insertion point or the active element.

By utilizing Zoom and adjusting its settings, users can magnify screen content to a comfortable level, making it easier to read text, view details, and interact with the iPhone's interface.

Navigating with AssistiveTouch

AssistiveTouch is an accessibility feature on the iPhone 15 Pro Max that provides an on-screen menu for accessing various functions, such as Home, Siri, Control Center, and more. It's particularly helpful for users who have difficulty performing certain gestures or require an alternative method of interaction.

To enable AssistiveTouch, go to Settings > Accessibility > Touch > AssistiveTouch and toggle the switch to "On." A semi-transparent button will appear on the screen, which you can drag to any edge of the screen for convenient access.

AssistiveTouch Menu:

- Home: Return to the Home screen.

- Siri: Activate Siri for voice commands.

- Control Center: Open Control Center for quick access to settings and toggles.

- Notifications: View your notifications.

- Device: Access device functions like volume control, lock screen, and multitasking.

- Customize: Add or remove actions from the AssistiveTouch menu.

AssistiveTouch Gestures:

- Single Tap: Open the AssistiveTouch menu.

- Double Tap: Perform the default action for the selected item.

- Long Press: Access additional options for the selected item.

AssistiveTouch Settings:

- Idle Opacity: Adjust the transparency of the AssistiveTouch button when not in use.

- AssistiveTouch Actions: Create custom actions to automate frequently used tasks.

- Pointing Devices: Connect an external pointing device, such as a mouse or trackpad, for enhanced control.

By utilizing AssistiveTouch, users can navigate the iPhone, access various functions, and perform actions without relying solely on touch gestures, making the device more accessible and adaptable to individual needs

Controlling Your iPhone with Switch Control

Switch Control is an accessibility feature on the iPhone 15 Pro Max that allows users with limited mobility to control the device using external switches, such as buttons, joysticks, or head trackers. It enables navigation, selection, and interaction without relying on touch gestures.

To enable Switch Control, go to Settings > Accessibility > Switch Control and toggle the switch to "On." You'll be guided through a setup process to connect external switches and configure their actions.

Switch Control Scanning:

- Auto Scanning: Automatically highlights items on the screen, allowing you to select them using a switch.

- Manual Scanning: Manually move the highlight using switches to select the desired item.

Switch Control Actions:

- Select Item: Activate the currently highlighted item.

- Next Item: Move the highlight to the next item.

- Previous Item: Move the highlight to the previous item.

- Home: Return to the Home screen.

- App Switcher: Open the App Switcher to switch between apps.

- Control Center: Open Control Center for quick access to settings and toggles.

Switch Control Settings:

- Switches: Add, remove, or configure external switches and assign actions to them.

- Scanning Style: Choose between automatic or manual scanning.

- Scanning Speed: Adjust the speed at which the highlight moves.

- Dwell Control: Set the time delay before a highlighted item is automatically selected.

By utilizing Switch Control and configuring it according to their needs, users with limited mobility can effectively control their iPhone, access various functions, and perform actions without relying on touch gestures, making the device more accessible and adaptable.

Discovering Additional Accessibility Features

Beyond the primary accessibility features like VoiceOver, Zoom, AssistiveTouch, and Switch Control, the iPhone 15 Pro Max offers a wide range of additional features to address various needs and preferences. Here are some notable examples:

1.Magnifier: The Magnifier app turns the iPhone into a digital magnifying glass, providing real-time magnification of objects in the physical world. It's particularly helpful for users with low vision or those who need to magnify objects for close-up tasks.

2. Speak Screen: Speak Screen reads aloud any text displayed on the screen, including websites, emails, and documents. It's useful for users with visual impairments or those who prefer auditory learning.

3. Closed Captions and SDH: Closed captions and SDH (Subtitles for the Deaf and Hard of Hearing) provide text transcriptions of audio content in videos and other media. This feature is essential for users with hearing impairments or those who prefer to read along with audio.

4. Audio Descriptions: Audio descriptions provide narration of visual elements in videos, such as scene changes, actions, and expressions. It's particularly helpful for users with visual impairments to better understand the context of visual media.

5. Mono Audio: Mono Audio combines the left and right audio channels into a single channel, ensuring that all sounds are played through both earbuds or speakers. This feature is beneficial for users with hearing impairments in one ear.

6. Background Sounds: Background Sounds play calming sounds, such as rain, ocean waves, or white noise, to mask distracting noises and create a more relaxing environment. It's helpful for users with sensory sensitivities or those who need to focus in noisy environments.

7.LED Flash for Alerts: LED Flash for Alerts uses the camera flash to provide a visual cue for incoming calls, notifications, or alarms. It's particularly useful for users with hearing impairments or those who prefer visual alerts.

8.Assistive Listening Devices: The iPhone supports pairing with assistive listening devices, such as hearing aids or cochlear implants, to enhance audio clarity and accessibility.

9.Voice Control: Voice Control allows users to control their iPhone entirely with voice commands, enabling navigation, selection, and interaction without relying on touch or switches.

10.Guided Access: Guided Access restricts the iPhone to a single app and limits certain features, preventing distractions and accidental interactions. It's helpful for users with cognitive or learning disabilities.

These are just a few examples of the extensive accessibility features available on the iPhone 15 Pro Max. By exploring these features and customizing them to individual needs, users can create a more inclusive and personalized mobile experience.

GLOSSARY

Here's a glossary of accessibility terms:

Accessibility: The practice of designing products, services, and environments to be usable by people with a wide range of abilities and disabilities.

Assistive Technology (AT): Any item, piece of equipment, software program, or product system that is used to increase, maintain, or improve the functional capabilities of individuals with disabilities.

Closed Captions: Text transcriptions of the audio content in videos and other media, including dialogue, sound effects, and speaker identification.

Cognitive Accessibility: Designing for users with cognitive or learning disabilities, such as dyslexia, ADHD, or autism.

Guided Access: An iOS feature that restricts the iPhone to a single app and limits certain features to prevent distractions and accidental interactions.

Hearing Accessibility: Designing for users with hearing impairments, such as providing captions, audio descriptions, and support for assistive listening devices.

Magnifier: An iOS app that turns the iPhone into a digital magnifying glass, providing real-time magnification of objects in the physical world.

Mono Audio: An iOS feature that combines the left and right audio channels into a single channel, ensuring that all sounds are played through both earbuds or speakers.

Motor Accessibility: Designing for users with limited dexterity or motor impairments, providing alternative methods of interaction beyond touch gestures.

Speak Screen: An iOS feature that reads aloud any text displayed on the screen, including websites, emails, and documents.

Switch Control: An iOS feature that allows users with limited mobility to control the device using external switches, such as buttons, joysticks, or head trackers.

Subtitles for the Deaf and Hard of Hearing (SDH): Similar to closed captions but may include additional information, such as sound effects descriptions or speaker identification.

Universal Design: The design of products and environments to be usable by all people, to the greatest extent possible, without the need for adaptation or specialized design.

Vision Accessibility: Designing for users with visual impairments, such as providing screen magnification, screen readers, and high-contrast color schemes.

Voice Control: An iOS feature that allows users to control their iPhone entirely with voice commands.

VoiceOver: An iOS screen reader that provides spoken descriptions of on-screen elements and enables interaction using gestures and voice commands.

Zoom: An iOS feature that magnifies the entire screen or a specific area, making text and details easier to see.

RESOURCES

Here are some valuable resources for accessibility information and support:

Apple Accessibility: Apple's official accessibility website provides comprehensive information on all the accessibility features available on iPhone, iPad, Mac, and Apple Watch.

Accessibility Support: Apple's dedicated support page for accessibility offers various resources, including guides, tutorials, and contact information for specialized support.

Disability.gov: A comprehensive website from the U.S. government that provides information and resources on a wide range of disabilities, including assistive technology, education, employment, and legal rights.

AFB (American Foundation for the Blind): A non-profit organization dedicated to providing resources and advocacy for people with vision loss.

Hearing Loss Association of America (HLAA): A non-profit organization that provides support, advocacy, and information for people with hearing loss.

National Federation of the Blind (NFB): A non-profit organization that advocates for the rights of blind Americans and provides resources and support for its members.

AbleGamers: A charity organization that focuses on improving accessibility in the gaming industry and providing resources for gamers with disabilities

www.ingramcontent.com/pod-product-compliance
Lightning Source LLC
Chambersburg PA
CBHW071239050326
40690CB00011B/2177